The Soul-Winner's Handy Guide

by Yan T. Wee

THE SOUL-WINNER'S HANDY GUIDE

First Edition	:	© 1998 by Y. T. Wee
Second Edition	:	© 1999 by Y. T. Wee
Third Edition	:	© 2003 by Y. T. Wee
Third Edition (Reprint)	:	© 2011 by Y. T. Wee

Special thanks to Jubina Seah, Christina Tan and Christine Margaret Marsh for their invaluable time and effort in proofreading this Handy Guide; to Jenny and Dolly Yeo for their gracious help and publication of this book; to Wong Shih Yaw for the illustrations provided; to Nancy Wee for the cover of the book; and to my co-laborer and fellow pastor, Pastor Jacob Tan, for all his help and assistance in making this book possible.

The author covets the understanding and forgiveness of those whom he may have quoted without giving due recognition as he could not recollect nor trace the sources he has taken from.

All Scriptures are taken from the Authorized King James' Version.

Printed in the Republic of Singapore.

ISBN: 981-04-8794-0

PREFACE

Like any pastor and soul-winner, the author looks for a Handy Guide to carry along so as to have some quick answers and biblical references to "... give an answer to every man that asketh you a reason of the hope that is in you... " (1 Pet 3:15) To this end is The Soul-Winner's Handy Guide written to aid the soul-winner in his task of bringing the lost to Christ. The objectives are as follows:

1)   To help the believer in understanding why he believes in what he believes so that he can, in turn, confidently lead another soul to the Lord.

2)   To aid in the imparting and transferring of knowledge and necessary skills in soul-winning through classroom teaching or personal discipling to those who desire to be "fishers of men" rather than "keepers of aquarium".

3)   To assist in personal soul-winning in every possible circumstance - after church services, in street tracting, or door-to-door witnessing.

4)   To be used as evangelistic literature to be loaned or given to seeking non-believers for their personal study to have a more accurate picture of the essence of Christianity.

The Handy Guide can be used in the following manner:

1)   To use the textual or pictorial presentations under the heading, "The Presentation in Personal Evangelism" to share the gospel or to use some familiar verses of each section under "The Plan in Personal Evangelism" to present systematically and progressively the plan of salvation. The first verse in each section is taken from the book of Romans or what is commonly known as "The Romans' Road".

2)   To encourage questions after the presentation of the gospel and to answer them with the aid of the Handy Guide as well as from your own personal experiences.

3)   To encourage the hearer to make a decision and to lead him to the Lord as simply and directly as possible.

The Soul-Winner's Handy Guide is written to "sharpen our axes", "provide the ammunition" and raise up effective soul-winners for this great and glorious work of personal evangelism in these Last Days.

In questions (1) & (40), the soul-winner is advised not to use all the points given as it is too time consuming. Instead, he should just share them sufficiently and adequately at the level of the prospect. For question (40) which is on Evolution, if the subject matter is too technical for the soul-winner, he may direct his more technical-savvy inquirer to read for himself.

The 'Notes' section is for the soul-winner to add materials relevant to his culture and customize resources according to his needs in soul-winning. It can include notes on other cults, Christian living, etc.

The author is an Independent Baptist by conviction and seeks, through the ministry of the printed page, to reach out to as many as possible for the gospel of Jesus Christ in these Last Days before His soon coming.

A drop of ink may make a million think.

In Humble Dedication

To God Almighty,
whose grace alone has made
this book possible;

To my beloved wife, Janet,
and our four lovely children,
Benjamin, Caleb, Gretal and Asher,
A most wonderful company
in this earthly journey of mine;

To the Members of
Shalom Baptist Church and
Shaddai Baptist Church,
for their constant love and care;

And to the Lone Soul-Winner who labors
undiscouraged and undeterred to give
the world the Gospel of
our Lord Jesus Christ.

CONTENTS

CONTENTS

CONTENTS

SIN

For all have sinned, and come short of the glory of God. - Rom 3:23

Therefore to him that knoweth to do good, and doeth it not, to him it is sin. - Jas 4:17

SEPARATION

For the wages of sin is death; but the gift of God is eternal life through Jesus Christ our Lord. - Rom 6:23

The wicked shall be turned into hell, and all the nations that forget God. - Psa 9:17

We are born in sin and spend our lives coping with the consequences.

SACRIFICE

But God commendeth his love toward us, in that, while we were yet sinners, Christ died for us. - Rom 5:8

And that he was buried, and that he rose again the third day according to the scriptures. - 1 Cor 15:4

SALVATION

Sirs, what must I do to be saved? And they said, Believe on the Lord Jesus Christ, and thou shalt be saved, and thy house. - Acts 16:30-31

For by grace are ye saved through faith; and that not of yourselves: it is the gift of God: Not of works, lest any man should boast. - Eph 2:8-9

God loved us when there was nothing good to be seen in us and nothing good to be said of us.

SECURITY

And I give unto them eternal life; and they shall never perish, neither shall any man pluck them out of my hand. - Jn 10:28

Who are kept by the power of God through faith unto salvation ready to be revealed in the last time. - 1 Pet 1:5

A SINNER'S PRAYER

Dear God, I know I am a sinner. Please forgive me of my sins and help me to forsake them. I thank you for sending the Lord Jesus Christ who died for my sins and rose again on the third day. Now, I accept the Lord Jesus Christ to be my Savior. Please help me to love and obey you from this day onwards. I thank you for saving me. In Jesus' name I pray. Amen.

Therefore if any man be in Christ, he is a new creature: old things are passed away; behold, all things are become new. - 2 Cor 5:17

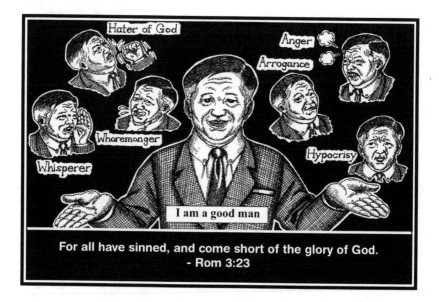

For all have sinned, and come short of the glory of God.
- Rom 3:23

And as it is appointed unto men once to die, but after this the judgment. - Heb 9:27

There is nothing more certain than death and nothing more uncertain than the time of death.

The wicked shall be turned into hell, and all the nations that forget God. - Psa 9:17

But God commendeth his love toward us, in that, while we were yet sinners, Christ died for us. - Rom 5:8

It does not require a decision to go to hell.

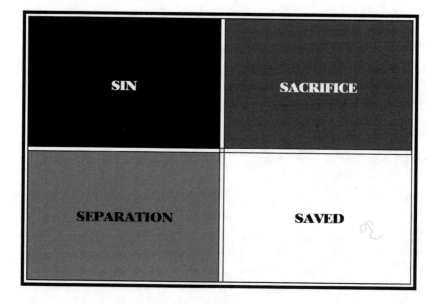

Nature forms us; sin deforms us; school informs us;
Christ transforms us.

1. **THE TEXTUAL PRESENTATION**

    a. The plan of salvation may be presented by using one or two verses given in each section.

2. **THE PICTORIAL PRESENTATION**

    a. The plan of salvation may be presented by using the combination of text and pictures.

    b. This section can be effectively used to share the gospel to those who may not understand the written language. By way of story-telling, one may show forth the plan of salvation.

3. **THE COLORED PRESENTATION**

    Like the "Wordless Book", one may share the plan of salvation by using the colors represented.

    a. **BLACK**   -   represents our sins.

    b. **ORANGE** -   represents the fire of hell.

    c. **RED**   -   represents the blood of Jesus Christ shed for our sins.

    d. **WHITE**   -   represents our new nature cleansed from our sins.

THE PROBLEM IN PERSONAL EVANGELISM

1. **HOW DO I KNOW THE BIBLE IS TRUE?**

    ### THE BIBLE IS SCIENTIFIC

    a. **IT SHOWS US THE EARTH IS ROUND:** It is he that sitteth upon the circle of the earth... Isa 40:22 (740-680 B.C.)

         Most ancient civilizations believed that the world was flat. Their mariners would not venture too far out into the oceans fearing that they would go over the "edge" into some unknown, fearsome abyss.

    b. **IT SHOWS US THE EARTH IS HANGING IN OUTER SPACE:** He stretcheth out the north over the empty place, and hangeth the earth upon nothing. - Job 26:7 (2000 B.C.)

        The majority of ancient traditions and legends would speak of the earth as being supported by huge pillars or on the back of some giant tortoise. When these moved, then you will have earthquakes.

    c. **IT SHOWS US THERE ARE UNDERSEA CURRENTS:** ... and whatsoever passeth through the paths of the seas. - Psa 8:8 (1410-430 B.C.)

        In 1885, Matthew Maury, a US Navy officer, after reading Psalm 8:8, set off to find these curious "paths of the seas." He eventually discovered these oceanic currents and came to be known as the "Pathfinder of the Seas".

    d. **IT SHOWS US THE ATMOSPHERE HAS WEIGHT:** To make the weight for the winds... - Job 28:25 (2000 B.C.)

        It was only in the 1600's that Galileo and his assistant, Evangelista Torricelli, discovered that air has weight.

e. **IT SHOWS US THE UNIVERSE IS RUNNING DOWN (THE SECOND LAW OF THERMODYNAMICS):** Of old hast thou laid the foundation of the earth: and the heavens are the work of thy hands. They shall perish, but thou shalt endure: yea, all of them shall wax old like a garment... - Psa 102:25-26 (1410-430 B.C.)

The sun and all the stars in the Universe are burning themselves out and the process is irreversible. The Universe, like a wound-up clock, is running down today. The question is: who raised the energy level so high as to make life possible? The Universe could have existed as darkness, and photosynthesis would not have been possible.

f. **IT SHOWS US THERE ARE TRILLIONS OF STARS IN OUTER SPACE:** That in blessing I will bless thee (Abraham), and in multiplying I will multiply thy seed as the stars of the heaven, and as the sand which is upon the sea shore; and thy seed shall possess the gate of his enemies. - Gen 22:17 (1450 B.C.)

As the host of heaven cannot be numbered, neither the sand of the sea measured... - Jer 33:22 (627-580 B.C.)

Before the invention of the telescope, man could only see, at the most, a few hundred stars with the naked eye. And yet the Bible knew of the trillions of stars out there in the Universe.

g. **IT SHOWS US THE UNIVERSE IS STILL EXPANDING:** Who coverest thyself with light as with a garment: who stretchest out the heavens like a curtain. - Psa 104:2 (1410-430 B.C.) / Thus saith God the LORD, he that created the heavens, and stretched them out... - Isa 42:5 (740-680 B.C.)

"The improved Hubble constant value 45.5 miles per second per megaparsec (A megaparsec equals 3.26 million light-years)." (NASA, NASA's Hubble Finds Universe Is Expanding Faster Than Expected, June 2nd 2016)

Scientists tell us that our universe is made up of protons, electrons, and neutrons. They forgot to mention morons.

h. IT SHOWS US THE EXISTENCE OF DAY AND NIGHT SIMULTANEOUSLY: Even thus shall it be in the day when the Son of man is revealed. **In that day,** he which shall be upon the housetop, and his stuff in the house, let him not come down to take it away: and he that is in the field, let him likewise not return back. Remember Lot's wife. Whosoever shall seek to save his life shall lose it; and whosoever shall lose his life shall preserve it. I tell you, **in that night** there shall be two men in one bed; the one shall be taken, and the other shall be left. - Lk 17:30-34 (58-63 A.D.)

The Bible predicted that when the Lord Jesus Christ comes again, it would be day in certain parts of the world and night in the other parts.

i. IT SHOWS US THERE ARE WATER FOUNTAINS UNDER THE OCEANS: Hast thou entered into the springs of the

sea? or hast thou walked in the search of the depth? - Job 38:16 (2,000 B.C.)

When he established the clouds above: when he strengthened the fountains of the deep. - Pro 8:28 (950-700 B.C.)

There are thousands of underwater volcanoes adding millions of metric tons of water into the oceans each year.

j. IT SHOWS US THE HYDROLOGIC CYCLE: All the rivers run into the sea; yet the sea is not full; unto the place from whence the rivers come, thither they return again. - Eccl 1:7 (950 B.C.)

The process of evaporation, condensation and precipitation of water was only discovered by Galileo in 1630.

k. IT SHOWS US LIGHT CAN BE PARTED: By what way is the light parted, which scattereth the east wind upon the earth? - Job 38:24 (2,000 B.C.)

People see God every day, they just don't recognize him.
- Pearl Bailey

White light, while passing through the prism, can be separated into seven colors. This was not understood until the 1600's.

I.   **IT SHOWS US THE SUN IS THE SOURCE OF THE EARTH'S WIND SYSTEM:** By what way is the light parted, **which scattereth the east wind upon the earth?** - Job 38:24

As the sun heats up the surface of the earth, it causes the hot air to rise and the cooler air to replace it. This creates the wind which we are so accustomed to. The Bible, years ahead of its time, knew the correlationship between the sun and the wind system.

m.   **IT SHOWS US THE WINDS DO BLOW IN CIRCUIT:** The wind goeth toward the south, and turneth about unto the north; it whirleth about continually, and the wind returneth again according to his circuits. - Eccl 1:6 (950 B.C.)

As the land in the equator heats up, it causes the hot air to rise. In the upper atmosphere, the air flows away from the equator. Cooler air will move along to replace it. This produces 6 major wind belts around the world.

n.   **IT SHOWS US THE EXISTENCE OF BACTERIA AND GERMS, AND THE PRACTICE OF QUARANTINE:** All the days wherein the plague shall be in him (the leper) he shall be defiled; he is unclean: he shall dwell alone; without (outside) the camp shall his habitation be. - Lev 13:46 (1444 B.C.)

Between 1347 and 1352, some 25 million people, more than one-third of the population of Europe died because of the Black Plague (Bubonic Plague). Many lives would not have been needlessly lost if only they knew of the existence of viruses and the practice of quarantine as taught in the Bible.

o. **IT SHOWS US THE REALITY OF ADAM AND EVE:** So God created man in his own image, in the image of God created he him; male and female created he them. And God blessed them, and God said unto them, Be fruitful, and multiply, and replenish the earth... - Gen 1:27-28 (1450 B.C.)

Mitochrondrial Eve: "To find Eve, Cann first had to persuade 147 pregnant women to donate their babies' placentas to science. The placentas were the easiest way to get large samples of body tissue. Working with Wilson and a Berkeley biologist, Mark Stoneking, Cann selected women in America with ancestors from Africa, Europe, the Middle East and Asia. Her collaborators in New Guinea and Australia found Aboriginal women there. The babies were born, the placentas were gathered and frozen, and the tissue analysis began at Wilson's lab in Berkeley... All the babies' DNA could be traced back, ultimately, to one woman." (John Tierney, Jan 11, 1998, Newsweek, Inc, All rights reserved. Reprinted with permission)

Y-Chromosome Adam: "In 1995, the journal Science published the results of a study in which a segment of the human Y-chromosome from 38 men from different ethnic groups were analyzed for variation (Dorit, R.L., Akashi, H. and Gilbert, W. 1995. "Absence of polymorphism at the ZFY locus on the human Y chromosome." Science 268:1183–1185). To their surprise, the researchers found no variation at all... Further research was done and it was determined that every man alive today actually descended from a single man who scientists now refer to as "Y-Chromosomal Adam"". (What are Y-Chromosomal Adam and Mitochondrial Eve, gotaquestion.org)

"...Now, two major studies of modern humans' Y chromosomes suggest that 'Y-chromosome Adam' and 'mitochondrial Eve' may have lived around the same time after all" (Poznik, G. D. et al. Science 341, 562–565, 2013).

My mind is made up, don't confuse me with facts.

p. **IT SHOWS US THE PRACTICE OF CIRCUMCISION ON THE EIGHTH DAY**: And he that is eight days old shall be circumcised among you, every man child in your generations... - Gen 17:12 (1450 B.C.)

"One simple aspect of God's command to Abraham helped prevent excessive bleeding with circumcision of the newborn. That was the instruction that the rite should be done on the eighth day of life. Modern medicine has come to understand the mechanisms at work in the clotting of blood. Of major importance in blood clotting is prothrombin, a compound made in the liver and the precursor of the active clotting agent thrombin. It has been well established that within a few hours after birth prothrombin becomes relatively depleted and does not become replenished by the infant's liver until about the eighth day of life". (Russel J. Thomsen, M.D., Medical Wisdom From the Bible, Old Tappan, New Jersey: Fleming H. Revell Company, 1974, pg 17)

q. **IT SHOWS US LIFE IS IN THE BLOOD**: For the life of the flesh is in the blood: and I have given it to you upon the altar to make an atonement for your souls: for it is the blood that maketh an atonement for the soul. - Lev 17:11 (1444 B.C.)

Blood is literally the life of the flesh as it carries oxygen, nutrients, etc throughout the whole body. Without it, the creature will die. It is ironical that in 1799, the US President, George Washington, died because of a common but wrong medical practice of his day - blood letting. It was believed then that some illnesses were caused by "bad blood", and by

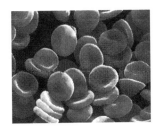

Red Blood Cells
Courtesy of Quill Graphics

cutting the veins to drain it out, the person would be healed. If only George Washington and the tens of thousands of his day had read Leviticus 17:11, they might have survived their illnesses. Sixty years after George Washington, this practice was still in use.

The foolish and the dead alone never change their opinions.
- James Russell Lowell

THE BIBLE IS PROPHETIC

a. **IT PREDICTED THE RETURN OF THE JEWS TO THEIR LAND BEFORE THE END OF THE WORLD**: "And it shall come to pass in that day, that the Lord shall set his hand again the second time to recover the remnant of his people, which shall be left, from Assyria, and from Egypt... And he shall... gather together the dispersed of Judah from the four corners of the earth." (Isa 11:11-12)

Israel palestine conflict

"... in the latter years thou shalt come into the land that is brought back from the sword, and is gathered out of many people, against the mountains of Israel, which have been always waste: but it is brought forth out of the nations..." (Ezek 38:8)

The Bible hinted that the world will not end until the Jews are first back in their own Land. Historically, because of their continuous disobedience toward God, the nation of Israel was destroyed and the Jews were scattered in 70 AD by the Romans. However, after World War II, on May 14, 1948, almost 2,000 years later, and against all odds, the Jews were given back their land by order of the United Nations. Israel earned the distinction of being the only people in the world who had been dispersed and re-gathered to their land after almost two millennia. All the present, on-going conflicts in the Middle East between the Israelis and the Palestinians are the results of this in-gathering of the Jews to Palestine in 1948.

On December 21, 1991, under Mikhail Gorbachev, the mighty Soviet Union (USSR) disintegrated to expedite the return of some 800,000 Russian Jews to Israel from behind the Iron Curtain. The world called it "an accident" but we know that God did it – "And I will bring you (the Jews) out from the people... with a mighty hand... and with fury poured out." (Ezek 20:34) In addition, between 1980 and 1991, approximately 85,000 Ethiopian Jews came back to their homeland in Israel. The Israeli population has grown from about 650,000 in 1948 to approximately 6 million today.

If you want a living proof of the reality of God, just look to Israel.

The Declaration of Israel's Independence

On May 14, 1948, against all odds, the modern state of Israel was reborn. At four o'clock that afternoon the members of the provisional national council, led by David Ben-Gurion, met in the Tel Aviv Art Museum. Ben-Gurion rose and read the following proclamation to the assembled guests:

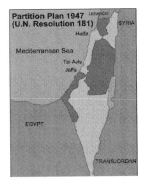

"The Land of Israel was the birthplace of the Jewish people. Here, the spiritual, religious and national identity was formed. Here, they achieved independence and created a culture of national and universal significance. Here, they wrote and gave the Bible to the world. Exiled from the Palestine, the Jewish people remained, faithful to it in all countries of their dispersion, never ceasing to pray and hope for their return and the restoration of their national freedom...

Accordingly we, the members of the National Council, representing the Jewish people in Palestine and the Zionist movement of the world, met together in solemn assembly today, the day of the termination of the British Mandate of Palestine, by virtue of the natural and historic right of the Jewish people and the Resolution of the General Assembly of the United Nations, hereby proclaim the establishment of the Jewish state in Palestine, to be called ISRAEL...

With trust in Almighty God, we set our hand to this declaration, at this session of the Provisional State Council, in the city of Tel Aviv, on this Sabbath eve, the fifth year of Iyar, 5708, the fourteenth day of May, 1948."

David Ben-Gurion reading the Declaration of Independence

b. **IT PREDICTED GOD WILL PRESERVE THE JEWS IN THEIR LAND DURING THE LAST DAYS:** And I will plant them upon their land, and they shall no more be pulled up out of their land which I have given them, saith the LORD thy God. - Amos 9:15 (824-810 B.C.)

From 1948 until today, the micro-state of Israel survived 5 major wars fought against her by her numerically superior neighbors. Three of these are:

The War of Independence in 1948, where 5 Arab nations - Syria, Lebanon, Jordan, Egypt and Iraq, simultaneously attacked Israel to destroy her at birth. The world did not give Israel much of a chance to survive, but miraculously, she not only survived, but enlarged her given territories.

General Shimon Erem said back in 1948: "Twenty thousand

untrained civilians, many of them speaking languages which could not be understood took on armies represented by 100 million Arabs, and prevailed. It was a miracle of God, there is no other explanation. God was keeping His word..."

The Six-Day War in 1967, where Israel, on the eve of a planned offensive by her Arab neighbors, launched a pre-emptive strike on June 5, destroying all the air forces of Iraq, Egypt, Syria and Jordan on the first day of the war before mopping up all their land forces within a 6-day period.

The Yom Kippur War in 1973, in which the combined Arab forces, through Egypt and Syria, launched a surprised attack and caught Israel flat-footed on the Day of Atonement - the holiest day in which the Jews were totally at rest. Israel was almost annihilated as the Syrian tanks and Egyptian forces steamrolled in the direction of Tel Aviv. For some unknown reason, the Arab forces hesitated and that break was sufficient for Israel to mobilize her military forces and launch a counter attack that brought her armies deep into Egypt and Syria before the UN intervened and stopped the war.

Revelation is not given to us for our entertainment but for our obedience.

Thus saith the LORD, which giveth the sun for a light by day, and the ordinances of the moon and of the stars for a light by night, which divideth the sea when the waves thereof roar; The LORD of hosts is his name: If those ordinances depart from before me, saith the LORD, then the seed of Israel also shall cease from being a nation before me for ever. - Jer 31:35-36 (627-580 B.C.)

c. **IT PREDICTED THE DISPERSED JEWS WILL COME BACK BY AIR AND SEA:** Who are these that fly as a cloud, and as the doves to their windows? Surely the isles shall wait for me, and the ships of Tarshish first, to bring thy sons from far, their silver and their gold with them, unto the name of the LORD thy God, and to the Holy One of Israel, because he hath glorified thee. - Isa 60:8-9

In May 1949, under Operation Magic Carpet, the Israeli aircrafts flew some 47,000 Yemenite Jews from Aden in Yemen to Israel. From the March of 1950, under Operation Ezra and Nehemiah, for 18 months, some 121,000 Iraqi Jews came back to Israel by air and sea.

d. **IT PREDICTED THE RETURNED JEWS WILL RECAPTURE THE HOLY CITY OF JERUSALEM:** Thus saith the LORD of hosts; Behold, I will save my people from the east country, and from the west country; And I will bring them, and they shall dwell in the midst of Jerusalem: and they shall be my people, and I will be their God, in truth and in righteousness. - Zech 8:7-8 (520 B.C.)

Jerusalem is the third most holy city to the Muslims after Mecca and Medina. Some think the miracle of the 6-Day War was that King Hussein of Jordan eventually decided to enter the war against his better judgment. By entering the war, Jordan lost Jerusalem to

Jerusalem

Israel on June 7, 1967, and this prophecy was fulfilled to the very letter - "... and Jerusalem shall be trodden down of the Gentiles, until the times of the Gentiles be fulfilled." (Lk 21:24)

e. IT PREDICTED THE LAND OF ISRAEL WILL TURN FROM A BARREN LAND INTO A FRUITFUL LAND: He shall cause them that come of Jacob to take root: Israel shall blossom and bud, and fill the face of the world with fruit. - Isa 27:6

Israel, which was largely a barren land for centuries before the return of the Jews, literally blossomed. Today, she is the third largest fruit-exporting country in the world. Even from satellite, one can see the greenery of Israel in stark contrast to the vast barrenness of her neighbors.

f. IT PREDICTED SOLOMON'S TEMPLE WILL BE REBUILT:

Who opposeth and exalteth himself above all that is called God, or that is worshipped; so that he as God sitteth in the temple of God, shewing himself that he is God. - 2 Thess 2:4 (55 A.D.)

The Dome of the Rock

The Moslem Mosque, the Dome of the Rock, now occupies the supposed site for Solomon's Temple. The Bible predicted, when the Anti-Christ comes, he will sit in the Temple of God and showing himself to be God.

The Temple Institute in Israel has prepared and fabricated most of the implements for the coming Third Temple. It is rumored that if the Dome of the Rock were to come down, the Temple will be raised within months.

Many believe the Anti-Christ, when he appears will, through diplomacy, achieve this near-impossible feat of getting the Temple built. Others believe the actual site for the Temple is somewhere away from the present Mosque and is on the site known as, "The Dome of the Tablets and the Spirits."

g. **IT PREDICTED JERUSALEM SHALL BE A CUP OF TREMBLING TO ALL THE NATIONS:** Behold, I will make Jerusalem a cup of trembling unto all the people round about, when they shall be in the siege both against Judah and against Jerusalem. And in that day will I make Jerusalem a burdensome stone for all people: all that burden themselves with it shall be cut in pieces, though all the people of the earth be gathered together against it. - Zech 12:2-3 (520 B.C.)

Some 2,500 years ago, Jerusalem was a wilderness in the days of the prophet Zechariah. And yet the Bible predicted that towards the end of the world, it will affect the peace of the whole world - what goes on in Jerusalem will be of great concern to the rest of the world.

"More than 60,000 individual votes have been cast in the UN against Israel. This tiny nation with one 1,000th of the world's population has occupied one-third of the United Nations' time — a burden indeed!" (Dave Hunt, Judgment Day)

h. **IT PREDICTED THE JEWS TODAY DO NOT HAVE ALL THE LANDS ORIGINALLY GIVEN BY GOD TO ABRAHAM:**

In the same day the LORD made a covenant with Abram, saying, Unto thy seed have I given this land, from the river of Egypt unto the great river, the river Euphrates. - Gen 15:18 (1450 B.C.)

I will also gather all nations, and will bring them down into the valley of Jehoshaphat, and will plead with them there for my people and for my heritage Israel, whom they have scattered among the nations, and parted my land. - Joel 3:2 (795-755 B.C.)

i. **IT PREDICTED THE PRESENT UNBELIEF OF THE RETURNED JEWS:** For I would not, brethren, that ye should be ignorant of this mystery, lest ye should be wise in your own conceits; that blindness in part is happened to Israel, until the fulness of the Gentiles be come in. And so all Israel shall be saved... - Rom 11:25-26 (58-60 A.D.)

 And I will pour upon the house of David, and upon the inhabitants of Jerusalem, the spirit of grace and of supplications: and they shall look upon me whom they have pierced, and they shall mourn for him, as one mourneth for his only son, and shall be in bitterness for him, as one that is in bitterness for his firstborn. - Zech 12:10 (520 B.C.) / So the house of Israel shall know that I am the LORD their God from that day and forward. - Ezek 39:22

Spiritually blinded, the Jews today are still looking for their coming Messiah. They failed to realize that He had already come - the Lord Jesus Christ whom their forefathers had rejected and crucified. Israel, as a nation, will be converted in the future Tribulation period.

j. **IT PREDICTED THE COMING "PEACE COVENANT" IN THE MIDDLE EAST:** And he shall confirm the covenant with many for one week: and in the midst of the week he shall cause the sacrifice and the oblation to cease, and for the overspreading of abominations he shall make it desolate, even until the consummation, and that determined shall be poured upon the desolate. - Dan 9:27

Since the return of the Jews to their Land, there has been no lasting peace between the Arab nations and Israel. Many attempts were made to solve the Israeli-Palestinian conflict, from the Rhodes Conference in 1949 to the Madrid Conference of 1991, the Oslo Accords in 1993, and of late, the 'Road Map to Peace' (2003) which was initiated by the United States and with the support of the United Nations, the European Union, and Russia (the so-called 'Middle East Quartet').

To God, prophecy is history written backwards.

"The Roadmap represents a starting point toward achieving the vision of two states, a secure State of Israel and a viable, peaceful, democratic Palestine. It is a framework for progress towards lasting peace and security in the Middle East..." (President George W. Bush)

This "tattered Road Map" was doomed to fail from the start as the real issue is one of ideology: the Arabs wanted the Jews out of the Land, and Israel intended to stay put. Besides, there were the complicated issues involving the ownership of Jerusalem, the final borders between the Israelis and the Palestinians, and the refugees' problems.

According to this prophecy of the Bible, some day in the future, the Anti-Christ will be able to successfully negotiate and seal this 'Peace Covenant' or, to some, the 'Covenant with Death', and in the middle of that 7-year peace treaty, he will betray Israel and seek to destroy her.

k. **IT PREDICTED THE COMING ONE-WORLD LEADER (THE ANTI-CHRIST) AND GOVERNMENT:** ... and power was given him over all kindreds, and tongues, and nations. And all that dwell upon the earth shall worship him, whose names are not written in the book of life of the Lamb... - Rev 13:7-8 (96 A.D.)

Towards the end of this age, countries all over the world will largely gravitate towards a "One-World Government" with a "One-World Leader" – the Anti-Christ. Presently, the political leaders of the world are awakening to the stark reality that their nations cannot survive in isolation. The onslaught of globalization, the new, borderless economy, the advent of the Internet, the possible environmental catastrophes facing mankind – global warming, ozone depletion, etc, and international conflicts and crises, which require multinational cooperative efforts to resolve, are inevitably forcing all these nations to come together in interdependence.

The Arabs have the oil but we have the matches.
- An Israeli Premier

The latest trend in the world is towards the concept of "The New World Order," "Globalization" and "Global Governance." The formation of international bodies like the UN (United Nations), WTO (World Trade Organization), ICJ (International Court of Justice) IMF (International Monetary Fund) and ICC (International Criminal Court) are systematically laying the groundwork for this coming New World Order. These, together with the formation of the Common Markets (NAFTA, EU & ASEAN), are drawing the nations of the world into a "One-World Government".

The world today is crying for a "someone" to take charge of the endless political, economical, social problems that are plaguing mankind. That someone will eventually appear on the horizon – the Anti-Christ, the greatest deceiver of all times – "Even him, whose coming is after the working of Satan with all power and signs and lying wonders, And with all deceivableness of unrighteousness in them that perish; because they received not the love of the truth, that they might be saved." (2 Thess 2:9-10)

The Advance of the New World Order:

(CBN): "With nation linked to nation through the economics of trade and the financial markets, and certain regions of the world almost perpetually on the brink of war, some believe there's a real need for world government. Author Gary Kah has researched groups which support global government. "I believe that we are quite possibly one major world crisis away from

 world government becoming a reality," says Kah. "I'm talking about either an economic crisis or a military crisis, or possibly a combination of both." Kah says war has often been associated with moves toward global government. The formation of the League of Nations followed World War I, and the United Nations was formed after World War II. The 1991 Gulf War brought a lot of popularity to the term "New World Order," a catch phrase often used by President George Bush."

Hell is a prepared place for an unprepared people.

"The Final Act of the Uruguay Round, marking the conclusion of the most ambitious trade negotiation of our century, will give birth - in Morocco - to the World Trade Organization, the third pillar of the New World Order, along with the United Nations and the International Monetary Fund." (Part of full-page advertisement by the government of Morocco in the New York Times; April 1994).

Richard A. Falk, in an article entitled "Towards a New World Order: Modest Methods and Drastic Visions," in the book "On the Creation of a Just World Order" (1975):

"The existing order is breaking down at a very rapid rate, and the main uncertainty is whether mankind can exert a positive role in shaping a new world order or is doomed to await collapse in a passive posture. We believe a new order will be born no later than early in the next century and that the death throes of the old and the birth pangs of the new will be a testing time for the human species."

Wiring the West, Steve Harris, May, 1999, The Age Melbourne:

For older heads like Lee Kuan Yew and Yehudi Menuhin, the rapidity of change, life at the speed of thought, is challenging man's ability to cope. Lee has masterminded the success of Singapore, a country whose technology, education and national unity is the envy of many a world leader. But even he is worried.

"The world is changing so fast I'm not sure Singapore can adjust fast enough to keep up and find a niche in the powerful knowledge-based economies," he said at Davos. "The speed with which societies are being interlinked to each other, the ease with which they can influence the other, will make for a totally new world. It may erode long-held values that have held our society together. I see signs of it already."

The new EU President, Herman Van Rompuy, has proclaimed 2009 as the "first year of global governance":

"We're living through exceptionally difficult times – the financial crisis and its dramatic impact on employment and budgets, the climate crisis which threatens our very survival, a period of anxiety, uncertainty and lack of confidence. Yet these problems can be overcome through a joint effort between our countries. 2009 is also the first year of global governance with the establishment of the G20 in the middle of the financial crisis. The climate conference in Copenhagen is another step toward the global management of our planet."

I. **IT PREDICTED THE COMING "MARK OF THE BEAST" (666):** And he causeth all, both small and great, rich and poor, free and bond, to receive a mark in their right hand, or in their foreheads: And that no man might buy or sell, save (except) he that had the mark, or the name of the beast, or the number of his name. - Rev 13:16-17

The Anti-Christ, when he appears in the coming Tribulation period, will cause everyone to have a particular mark in their right hands or foreheads in order to buy or sell. This technology to control the world's commerce is already at our doorstep – the Human ID Implant or the RFID (radio frequency identification) tags.

Presently, we are heading towards a cashless system where eventually all economic transactions may be made through the microchips, implanted in our right hands or on our foreheads. The "plastic card" (ATM, VISA, MASTERCARD, etc.) is the intermediate medium which may eventually lead to the use of microchips. Already, in the USA, microchips are implanted in dogs and cats so that their owners can be located when they (the pets) go astray. Generally, people are wary of any form of the "Big Brother Program", but with the destruction of the World Trade Center in New York, USA, on September 11, 2001, the American government, in

The Devil's greatest lie: we still have time.

the fight against terrorism, is apparently pushing for some form of universal identification of her citizens with the use of microchip technology. Today, national security supercedes personal privacy. However, we are not exactly sure of the final version of this "Mark of the Beast" – the implanted microchips could be just one step away from it.

AP, February, 2002, "Answer to Security Prayer? – Human ID-chip implants", it states:

"Sept 11 catapults security industry into an era of uncharted possibilities - not to mention a human-rights minefield.

WASHINGTON - Embedding a computer chip the size of a long grain of rice beneath a person's skin could be the answer to a need for foolproof security at vital installations.

A Florida technology company is poised to ask the government for permission to market a first-ever computer ID chip that could be inserted under the skin for use at airports, nuclear power plants and other high-security facilities. But privacy advocates warn the chip 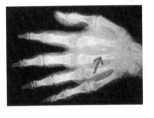 could lead to encroachment on civil liberties. The implant technology is another case of science fiction evolving into fact.

Other uses of the technology on the horizon, from an added device that would allow satellite-tracking of an individual's every movement to the storage of medical records and other sensitive data, are already attracting interest across the globe for tasks such as foiling kidnappings or helping paramedics.

Applied Digital, based in Palm Beach, Florida, says it will soon begin the process of getting Food and Drug Administration's approval for the device..."

"How'd you like to avoid waiting in lines for the rest of your life? Breeze through everywhere like you owned the place. Watch lights snap on, doors open automatically, money pop out of ATMs as you approach. Never have to show an ID, buy a ticket, carry keys, remember a password. You'd leave stores loaded with packages and waltz right past the cashiers. You wouldn't have to carry a wallet. Ever. Family and friends could find you instantly in any crowd. There's only one catch—you'd need to have a tiny little chip implanted in your body. No big deal..." (Paul Somerson, "Inside Job", PC Computing, Oct. 1999, p. 87)

"Most likely. . . it would be implanted on the back of the right or left hand for convience, so that it would be easy to scan." (Marin Independent Journal, April 2, 1989 p. A10)

Time magazine, April 27, 1998, pp. 50,51:

A single electronic card may replace everything in your wallet including...

... your cash
... your credit cards
... your ATM card
... your ID cards
... your insurance
... and your life

FUTURE: One card, or one chip, with your life on it.

The Straits Times, Singapore, March 26, 1998 states:

In 10 years you will have... a chip in your head

Take out your wallet and count the number of cards you carry, not to mention all the Personal Identification Numbers (PINs) that you have to memorize for every possible transaction...

Everything from employment and medical records to financial status can be written into the chip. Add a short-range wireless transmitter-receiver, implant the whole thing

Hell is an abiding place, but no resting place.

under your skin, and you have a personal transponder, just like those in aeroplanes... Even grocery-shopping could be easier. Just walk into a store and pick up whatever you want to buy. No more queues at the cashier's counter. All this could be a reality in 10 years' time. (used with permission from the Straits Times)

THE STRAITS TIMES

Fast Forward

No more cards, just a chip in your head

Yes, no more worries about PIN numbers and other personal details.

Everything can be stored in a chip implanted under your skin, in your head. This is not sci-fi, but something that can come about in 10 years' time, says BT Laboratories' Peter Cochrane.

Cover Story
PAGES 2 and 3

Photo illustration by DOMENIC WONG

m. **IT PREDICTED THE SPEED OF TRAVEL AND THE EXPONENTIAL INCREASE IN KNOWLEDGE IN THE END TIMES:**

But thou, O Daniel, shut up the words, and seal the book, even to the time of the end: many shall run to and fro, and knowledge shall be increased. - Dan 12:4

The Bible predicted that in the Last Days, many people would be traveling to and fro at incredible speed and there would be an explosion of knowledge. In the last 5,000 years of observable, human history, technology has hardly changed – man lived off the land and the fastest speed he could travel was on horseback. But in the last 100 years or so, we are communicating with the speed of light and traveling

It is never true to say that something 'hurts like hell'.
Nothing hurts like hell.

past the speed of sound. The Twentieth Century alone saw the invention of cars, trains, planes, radio, television, satellites, rockets, computers, the internet, et al. Knowledge is estimated to be doubling every two years. Technology is moving so fast that what's new today will be obsolete in a short while.

Hurried Century

(AP) The Twentieth Century. It started with horses and hours. It ends with Maseratis and microseconds, with cars speeding across highways, airplanes streaking across skies, microprocessors burning across desktops and space shuttles circling the earth. This century's mad dash of innovation has produced all of these things - and the most frantic human era ever.

We phone. We fax. We page. We e-mail. We race from one end of life to the other, rarely glancing over our shoulders. Technology, mass media and a desire to do more, do it better and do it yesterday have turned us into a world of "hurriers".

1908: the Ford Model T, top speed 45 mph.

1933: the Boeing 247 (600 miles in four hours).

1947: test pilot Chuck Yeager breaks the sound barrier (700 mph).

1969: Apollo 10's three astronauts become the fastest humans ever (24,791 mph).

"No century has been like this. And we're only speeding up," says David Grubin, producer of the recent PBS documentary "America 1900."

There are two places the jet planes have brought closer together
- this world and the next.

n. IT PREDICTED THE DRYING UP OF THE RIVER EUPHRATES AND THE BATTLE OF ARMAGEDDON:

And the sixth angel poured out his vial upon the great river Euphrates; and the water thereof was dried up, that the way of the kings of the east might be prepared... which go forth unto the kings of the earth and of the whole world, to gather them to the battle of that great day of God Almighty... into a place called in the Hebrew tongue Armageddon.
- Rev 16:12-16

The Ataturk Dam

The Bible tells us that towards the end of the Tribulation period, the River Euphrates will dry up to allow an assemblage of formidable armies from the East (possibly China, etc) to cross into Israel for the last great battle – the Battle of Armageddon, the Mother of all Battles, where all the great armies of the world will converge. However, many Messianic Jews believe that these armies from the East will consist of the Islamic countries of Pakistan, Afghanistan, and the breakaway countries from the previous Soviet bloc - Kazakhstan, Uzbekistan, Tajikistan, et al.

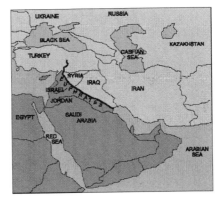

Turkey has built one of the world's largest dams - the Ataturk Dam on the River Euphrates. On January 13, 1990, she began to fill the reservoirs behind the giant Ataturk Dam. Anticipating her neighbors' complaints, the Turks increased the water flow 50% before cutting it down to a trickle. Both Iraq and Syria protested to no avail. Today, it is possible to "dry up" this huge, gigantic river - the River Euphrates.

Facts about the Anatolia Project (GAP):

"The Euphrates River, or the Furat in Arabic and Turkish, flows from its origins in Turkey through Syria and into Iraq.

Turkey's Southeast Anatolia Project, known by the Turkish acronym GAP, is causing concern in Syria and Iraq about the future of their access to the waters of the Euphrates. GAP, a concept as early as the 1930's, was begun in 1997. The project includes more than 20 dams and 17 electric power plants, which will eventually supply over half of Turkey's electricity requirements. However, filling the reservoirs behind these dams will reduce the flow of water downstream to Syria and Iraq."

o. **IT PREDICTED THE INVENTION OF TELEVISION AND SATELLITES:**

And I will give power unto my two witnesses, and they shall prophesy a thousand two hundred and threescore days (1,260 days)... And when they shall have finished their testimony, the beast that ascendeth out of the bottomless pit shall make war against them, and shall overcome them, and kill them. And their dead bodies shall lie in the street of the great city... where also our Lord was crucified. **And they of the people and kindreds and tongues and nations shall see their dead bodies three days and an half, and shall not suffer (allow) their dead bodies to be put in graves...** And after three days and an half the Spirit of life from God entered into them, and they stood upon their feet; and great fear fell upon them which saw them. - Rev 11:3-11 (96 A.D.

In the Tribulation Period, God will send two prophets to prophesy against the world for three and a half years. After that, the Anti-Christ will be allowed to kill these two prophets and the whole world will be able to view their bloodied bodies in Jerusalem within a three-and-a-half day period. This is only possible through a live telecast of the event with the aid of television and satellites.

We are called to be soul-seekers, not sign-seekers.

THE END TIMES PROGRAM

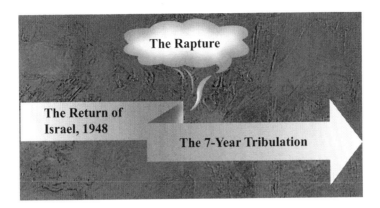

The Rapture

For the Lord himself shall descend from heaven with a shout, with the voice of the archangel, and with the trump of God: and the dead in Christ shall rise first: Then we which are alive and remain shall be caught up together with them in the clouds, to meet the Lord in the air: and so shall we ever be with the Lord. - 1 Thess 4:16-17

The Tribulation

For then shall be great tribulation, such as was not since the beginning of the world to this time, no, nor ever shall be. - Mt 24:21

And the kings of the earth, and the great men, and the rich men, and the chief captains, and the mighty men, and every bondman, and every free man hid themselves in the dens and in the rocks of the mountains... For the great day of his wrath is come; and who shall be able to stand? - Rev 6:15-17

2. I CANNOT SEE GOD.

a. We can believe in the invisible Creator by seeing the visible things He has created.

   i. **FROM CAUSE AND EFFECT:** All things were made by him; and without him was not any thing made that was made. - Jn 1:3

   The Universe is a vacuum. Where then did matter and energy come from? Who placed the sun, moon and the constellations of stars in the outer space? Other than God Himself, something cannot come from nothing.

   ii. **FROM DESIGN AND INTELLIGENCE:** For the invisible things of him from the creation of the world are clearly seen, being understood by the things that are made, even his eternal power and Godhead; so that they are without excuse. - Rom 1:20

   Gravity will draw two body masses together while the same pole of two magnets coming together will repel. Water, when cooled, will contract until it reaches 4 degree Celsius, after which, it will expand. This property of water causes the lakes during winter to remain unfrozen beneath the surface and allows the fishes to survive. Two atoms of hydrogen when covalently bonded with one atom of oxygen will give us water (H_2O). Who laid down all these "invisible laws" of physics and chemistry that harmonized together in such a wonderful and intricate way to make life possible?

   By looking at the watch, we know that the watchmaker exists even though we have not seen him. Likewise, by looking at the complexity, beauty and orderliness in creation, we can know of the existence of an intelligent Creator even though we have not seen Him.

   iii. In the beginning God created the heaven and the earth. - Gen 1:1 This is the most scientific statement about how this intricate world came into existence.

All that I can see points to Him whom I cannot see.

b. Even if we can see God we may not automatically believe in Him.

  i. **MAN HAS REJECTED GOD:** Because that which may be known of God is manifest in them; for God hath shewed (shown) it unto them. For the invisible things of him from the creation of the world are clearly seen... Because that, when they knew God, they glorified him not as God, neither were thankful; but became vain in their imaginations, and their foolish heart was darkened. Professing themselves to be wise, they became fools. - Rom 1:19-22

  ii. **MAN HAS REJECTED THE TRUTH:** And this is the condemnation, that light is come into the world, and men loved darkness rather than light, because their deeds were evil. For every one that doeth evil hateth the light, neither cometh to the light, lest his deeds should be reproved. - Jn 3:19-20

  iii. Man will not go to God for the same reason a thief will not go to a policeman.

  iv. Man is a peculiar, puzzling paradox, groping for God and hoping to hide from him at the selfsame time. - William A. Ward

3. **I CANNOT UNDERSTAND EVERYTHING ABOUT THE BIBLE.**

  a. We make use of many things we do not fully understand.

  i. We do not understand everything about medicine or electricity, and yet we use them. Imagine a dying man saying to a doctor, "Doctor, since I cannot understand everything about medicine, I will not take it."

  b. We can understand our need to be saved from hell.

  i. <u>We have sinned:</u> The Bible teaches it, our conscience attests to it, and our experience confirms it.

  For all have sinned, and come short of the glory of God. - Rom 3:23

The Bible is like a mirror - it shows us who we are and not what we think we are.

ii. <u>We will be judged:</u> As moral beings, we judge one another all the time. One day, we will be judged by a Perfect and Moral God.

And as it is appointed unto men once to die, but after this the judgment. - Heb 9:27

iii. <u>We cannot save ourselves:</u> We keep falling into sins and can never be perfect, no matter how much or hard we try.

For there is not a just man upon earth, that doeth good, and sinneth not. - Eccl 7:20

iv. <u>We will be sent to hell:</u> A perfect God hates sins thoroughly and will send the sinner to hell forever.

The wicked shall be turned into hell, and all the nations that forget God. - Psa 9:17

v. <u>We can be saved by faith through Jesus Christ who died for us:</u> Jesus Christ is God who came to die in our place as a sinless sacrifice for our sins.

But God commendeth his love toward us, in that, while we were yet sinners, Christ died for us. - Rom 5:8

For by grace are ye saved through faith; and that not of yourselves: it is the gift of God: Not of works, lest any man should boast. - Eph 2:8-9

c. Someone once commented, "It is not what I don't understand that bothers me. It is what I do understand that bothers me - I am a sinner without hope on my way to hell."

d. "Many things in the Bible I cannot understand; many things in the Bible I only think I understand; but there are many things in the Bible I cannot misunderstand." (Moody Monthly)

e. The man with cancer needs first to know how he can be cured from cancer. All other knowledge is secondary. Likewise, the sinner needs first to know how he can be saved from Hell.

Men do not reject the Bible because they find faults in it, but because it finds faults in them. - Paul Hovey

4. WHY WOULD A LOVING GOD SEND A SOUL TO HELL FOREVER?

a. God is a God of supreme love.

   i. For God so loved the world, that he gave his only begotten Son, that whosoever believeth in him should not perish, but have everlasting life. - Jn 3:16

   ii. Greater love hath no man than this, that a man lay down his life for his friends. - Jn 15:13

b. God is also a God of justice.

   i. Justice and judgment are the habitation of thy throne... - Psa 89:14

   ii. A nation has justice when her criminals are punished in accordance to the law for their crimes. A nation has no justice when every crime is excused and every criminal is freed. Likewise, God's justice demands that every sinner be punished accordingly.

c. The more perfect and righteous we are, the more we will hate sins. God is one hundred percent perfect and holy, and He hates sins thoroughly. No sinner can dwell in His holy presence and He will send every sinner into hell forever.

   i. For thou art not a God that hath pleasure in wickedness: neither shall evil dwell with thee. The foolish shall not stand in thy sight: thou hatest all workers of iniquity. Thou shalt destroy them that speak leasing (falsehood): the LORD will abhor the bloody and deceitful man. - Psa 5:4-6

   ii. The wicked shall be turned into hell, and all the nations that forget God. - Psa 9:17

   iii. And these shall go away into everlasting punishment: but the righteous into life eternal. - Mt 25:46

   iv. "The very animals whose smell is most offensive to us have no idea that they are offensive, and are not offensive to one another. And man, fallen man, has just no idea what a vile thing sin is in the sight of God." (J. C. Ryle)

Those who demand nothing more than a God of justice get precisely what they ask; the Bible calls it hell.

d. When a person dies, his character is fixed. This is another reason why hell is forever.

    i. He that is unjust, let him be unjust still: and he which is filthy, let him be filthy still: and he that is righteous, let him be righteous still: and he that is holy, let him be holy still. - Rev 22:11

    This verse is true only in the light of eternity where the human character becomes fixed.

    ii. Death stamps the characters and conditions of men for eternity. As death finds them in this world, so will they be in the next world. - Nathaniel Emmons

e. God does not desire to see any soul in hell.

    i. Have I any pleasure at all that the wicked should die? saith the Lord GOD: and not that he should return from his ways, and live? - Ezek 18:23

    ii. The Lord is not slack concerning his promise, as some men count slackness; but is longsuffering to us-ward, not willing that any should perish, but that all should come to repentance. - 2 Pet 3:9

5. THERE IS NO SUCH THING AS SIN - EVERYTHING IS RELATIVE.

a. Some things in life are relative.

    i. Depending on the circumstances, the one who kills can be either a murderer or an executioner. However, some things in life are absolute: the one who kills because of greed is a murderer, while the one who kills because of justice as required by the State is an executioner.

b. Some things in life are absolute.

    i. Those who have convinced themselves that everything is relative still get mad at the wrongs done to them - when someone robs their homes, hurts them or kills their loved ones. Why? Because they, in their hearts, still believe in absolutes - that these crimes are morally wrong. They would not smile at such injustices done to them and explain these injustices away as, "everything is relative."

c. In reality, those who advocate the idea that "everything is relative" just want to enjoy their sins without being made to feel guilty.

   i. Being filled with all unrighteousness, fornication, wickedness, covetousness, maliciousness; full of envy, murder, debate, deceit, malignity; whisperers, Backbiters, haters of God, despiteful, proud, boasters, inventors of evil things, disobedient to parents... Who knowing the judgment of God, that they which commit such things are worthy of death, not only do the same, but have pleasure in them that do them. - Rom 1:29-32

d. **FOOD FOR THOUGHT:**

   Question: Do you believe that everything is relative and nothing is absolute?

   Answer: Yes!

   Question: Is that an absolute statement?

   Answer: Yes!

   Question: But, I thought you just said that there is nothing absolute?

6. **I AM SINCERELY DOING THE BEST THAT I CAN.**

   a. Sincerity and truth are not identical. Sincerity is sincerity and truth is truth. Sincerity without truth is sincerely wrong.

      i. If, by accident, we board the wrong bus, will our sincerity and faith in that bus amount to anything? Will it bring us to our destination? So likewise, sincerity without truth is sincerely wrong.

      ii. In life, there are numerous examples of people who were sincerely wrong: hospital patients who sincerely trusted in their physicians and died because of wrong or overdosed medication, or airplane passengers who sincerely placed their faith in the aircraft they were traveling in and never made it to their destinations due to some mishaps. There is nothing great about sincerity if it lacks the truth.

b. The Jews were sincere in going about to establish their own righteousness, and yet, they were sincerely lost in their sins.

    i. Brethren, my heart's desire and prayer to God for Israel is, that they might be saved. **For I bear them record that they have a zeal of God, but not according to knowledge. For they being ignorant of God's righteousness, and going about to establish their own righteousness, have not submitted themselves unto the righteousness of God.** For Christ is the end of the law for righteousness to every one that believeth. For Moses describeth the righteousness which is of the law, That the man which doeth those things shall live by them. But the righteousness which is of faith speaketh on this wise... That if thou shalt confess with thy mouth the Lord Jesus, and believe in thine heart that God hath raised him from the dead, thou shalt be saved. - Rom 10:1-9

    ii. What shall we say then? That the Gentiles, which followed not after righteousness, have attained to righteousness, even the righteousness which is of faith. **But Israel, which followed after the law of righteousness, hath not attained to the law of righteousness. Wherefore? Because they sought it not by faith, but as it were by the works of the law.** For they stumbled at that stumblingstone. - Rom 9:30-32

c. What saves a soul is not sincerity alone but sincerity coupled with the truth.

    i. ... Sirs, what must I do to be saved? And they said, Believe on the Lord Jesus Christ, and thou shalt be saved, and thy house. - Acts 16:30-31

    ii. And ye shall know the truth, and the truth shall make you free. - Jn 8:32

We are not saved by sincerity, but we may certainly be lost through insincerity. - Robert Black

7. **I CAN MAKE IT TO HEAVEN BY MY GOOD WORKS.**

a. In order to be saved by good works, we must keep all the laws of God without breaking any one of them. The breaking of just one law will render us guilty.

   i.   For as many as are of the works of the law are under the curse: for it is written, Cursed is every one that continueth not in all things which are written in the book of the law to do them. But that no man is justified by the law in the sight of God, it is evident: for, The just shall live by faith. - Gal 3:10-11

   ii. To be saved by good works or the keeping of the laws is like a man clinging on to a chain and hanging over a cliff. The chain is as good as each link. One broken link will send the man down the precipice to his death. One sin is enough to send the sinner into hell for ever.

   iii. For whosoever shall keep the whole law, and yet offend in one point, he is guilty of all. - Jas 2:10

   iv. Technically, most criminals have kept all the laws of the country and have broken just a couple of them. Yet, they are guilty before society.

   v.   The most unfair way to be saved is salvation by works because nobody is going to be saved. - Adapted

b. In reality, good works cannot wash away our sins.

   i.   I said therefore unto you, that ye shall die in your sins: for if ye believe not that I am he, ye shall die in your sins. - Jn 8:24

   ii. Imagine a robber who stole from a bank and, after feeling bad about it, decided to give away all his fortunes to the poor. What will happen when the law finally catches up with him? Will it say that since he has done such a noble and charitable deed, he should be forgiven? Of course not! Likewise, judicially speaking, good works cannot wash away our sins.

c. Nobody in the world can do good perfectly.

    i. For there is not a just (righteous) man upon earth, that doeth good, and sinneth not. - Eccl 7:20

    ii. For the good that I would I do not: but the evil which I would not, that I do... I find then a law, that, when I would do good, evil is present with me... O wretched man that I am! who shall deliver me from the body of this death? - Rom 7:19-24

e. We are saved by grace through our faith in Christ and not by depending on our good works.

    i. ... Sirs, what must I do to be saved? And they said, Believe on the Lord Jesus Christ, and thou shalt be saved, and thy house. - Acts 16:30-31

    ii. For by grace are ye saved through faith; and that not of yourselves: it is the gift of God: Not of works, lest any man should boast. - Eph 2:8-9

    iii. And if by grace, then is it no more of works: otherwise grace is no more grace. But if it be of works, then is it no more grace: otherwise work is no more work. - Rom 11:6

    iv. For therein is the righteousness of God revealed from faith to faith: as it is written, The just shall live by faith. - Rom 1:17

    v. If a man were to owe a creditor a hundred million dollars, and he can never in his lifetime repay that debt, then, the only logical option left is for someone else to help him pay that debt, and for him to freely receive with gratitude that generous help. Similarly, we can never repay our debts of sins and therefore, the only possible recourse left for us is for God to pay for our sins, and for us to freely receive by faith this gift of eternal life - "... the gift of God is eternal life through Jesus Christ our Lord." (Rom 6:23)

    vi. Salvation is a gift to be received, not a goal to be achieved.

Perfection demands perfection; that is why salvation must be by grace, and why works are not sufficient. - Donald Grey Barnhouse

8. DOESN'T SALVATION BY FAITH SOUND TOO EASY?

a. In life, everything we do or refuse to do is due to our "faith" or innermost beliefs.

    i. The reason why we want to make more money and lead a comfortable life is because we believe that it is good for us. The reason why we do not want to be poor or suffer hardship is because we believe that it is not good for us. All our thinking, attitudes, behaviors and actions are shaped and determined by our innermost beliefs or faith. This is why God would rather focus on our belief or faith than on our external works.

    ii. In reality, it is harder to believe than to work. Also, we can do many things in life without believing (like pleasing our bosses), but we cannot believe without doing (like giving our best to our loved ones).

b. If God were to focus on our external works, then we would end up doing good works perfunctorily or artificially without any real personal conviction.

    i. We can become hypocritical by doing good works to ease our conscience or to make an impression on others.

    ii. But all their works they do for to be seen of men... - Mt 23:5

    iii. Woe unto you, scribes and Pharisees, hypocrites! for ye make clean the outside of the cup and of the platter, but within they are full of extortion and excess... Woe unto you, scribes and Pharisees, hypocrites! for ye are like unto whited sepulchres (graves), which indeed appear beautiful outward, but are within full of dead men's bones, and of all uncleanness. Even so ye also outwardly appear righteous unto men, but within ye are full of hypocrisy and iniquity. - Mt 23:25-28

c. A true, saving faith will result in us doing the works of God.

    i. By faith Noah, being warned of God of things not seen

Without faith, God can do nothing with man, and man can do nothing with God.

41

as yet, moved with fear, prepared an ark to the saving of his house... By faith Abraham, when he was called to go into a place which he should after receive for an inheritance, obeyed; and he went out, not knowing whither he went. - Heb 11:7-8

ii. We are saved by faith without works, but never by a faith that is without works - "Even so faith, if it hath not works, is dead, being alone." (Jas 2:17)

iii. Faith and works are like the light and heat of a candle; they cannot be separated.

iv. Faith is like the root of which work is the fruit.

d. Because we are saved by faith we can be free to love and obey God.

   i. Therefore being justified by faith, we have peace with God through our Lord Jesus Christ. - Rom 5:1

   ii. And ye shall know the truth, and the truth shall make you free. - Jn 8:32

   iii. If we were to be saved by good works, then we would have to keep on keeping on without any assurance that we would make it. It would be like a burden we carry and could not be put down. The real motivation for our good works would be more out of fear than of love. We were afraid that we would not make it. Whereas, because we are saved by faith through the perfect and sinless sacrifice of God for us, the Lord Jesus Christ, we will never be in hell - not because we are good or perfect but because of Christ's goodness and perfection. He died in our place and paid the penalty of our sins. This truly sets us free to love and obey Him.

   iv. "There is a great difference between your religion and mine," said a Christian to his neighbor. "Indeed!" was the reply. "What is that?" "It is this: Yours has only two letters in it, while mine has four." "What do you mean?" said he. "Well, yours has 'DO'. Mine has 'DONE'."

Religion says, "Do and live." Christianity says, "Live and do."

9. WHY IS CHRISTIANITY THE ONLY WAY TO GOD?

a. Religion is basically man's attempt to reach God, and it is hopeless.

   i. **THROUGH GOOD WORKS:** The Pharisee stood and prayed thus with himself, God, I thank thee, that I am not as other men are, extortioners, unjust, adulterers, or even as this publican. I fast twice in the week, I give tithes of all that I possess... for every one that exalteth himself shall be abased; and he that humbleth himself shall be exalted. - Lk 18:11-14

    Those who seek to be justified by their good works will be condemned by their good works - because their good works will never be good enough - "For whosoever shall keep the whole law, and yet offend in one point, he is guilty of all." (Jas 2:10)

   ii. **THROUGH SELF-RIGHTEOUSNESS:** They say unto him, Master, this woman was taken in adultery, in the very act. Now Moses in the law commanded us, that such should be stoned: but what sayest thou? This they said, tempting him, that they might have to accuse him. But Jesus... said unto them, He that is without sin among you, let him first cast a stone at her... And they which heard it, being convicted by their own conscience, went out one by one, beginning at the eldest, even unto the last... - Jn 8:4-9

    As it is written, There is none righteous, no, not one. - Rom 3:10

   iii. **THROUGH THE KEEPING OF THE LAWS OF GOD:** For as many as are of the works of the law are under the curse: for it is written, Cursed is every one that continueth not in all things which are written in the book of the law to do them. But that no man is justified by the law in the sight of God, it is evident: for, The just shall live by faith. - Gal 3:10-11

Religion is the fig leaf which man uses to try to cover his spiritual nakedness.

The system of the Law is such that either we keep all the laws or we are guilty of them all - "For whosoever shall keep the whole law, and yet offend in one point, he is guilty of all." (Jas 2:10)

The law of God is like a mirror; it can reveal flaws, but not remove them.

b. Christianity is God's attempt to reach man. This is man's only hope to be with God.

   i. **IT IS THROUGH HIS SON:** For God so loved the world, that he gave his only begotten Son, that whosoever believeth in him should not perish, but have everlasting life. For God sent not his Son into the world to condemn the world; but that the world through him might be saved. - Jn 3:16-17

   But God commendeth his love toward us, in that, while we were yet sinners, Christ died for us. - Rom 5:8

   But we see Jesus, who was made a little lower than the angels for the suffering of death, crowned with glory and honour; that he by the grace of God should taste death for every man. - Heb 2:9

   ii. **IT IS A GIFT OF GOD:** For by grace are ye saved through faith; and that not of yourselves: it is the gift of God: Not of works, lest any man should boast. - Eph 2:8-9

   The weakest hand can receive a precious gem.

   Salvation is free, but it cost the blood of the Lord Jesus Christ.

   iii. **IT IS SURE:** In hope of eternal life, which God, that cannot lie, promised before the world began. - Tit 1:2

   These things have I written unto you that believe on the name of the Son of God; that ye may know that ye have eternal life... - 1 Jn 5:13

A true gift is freely given and freely received.

Salvation is sure because it is a gift. Whereas, if it was a matter of works, then no one could be sure of getting saved.

iv. **IT IS JUST**: Being justified freely by his grace through the redemption that is in Christ Jesus: Whom God hath set forth to be a propitiation (conciliation) through faith in his blood, to declare his righteousness for the remission (forgiveness) of sins that are past, through the forbearance of God; **To declare, I say, at this time his righteousness: that he might be just, and the justifier of him which believeth in Jesus.** - Rom 3:24-26

In order for God to be just or righteous, sin must be paid for. We cannot pay for our sins and the Lord Jesus Christ came to die on the cross to pay for our sins with His blood. This is the only way in which God can be both "just, and the justifier of him which believeth in Jesus." Through this, God's justice is upheld, sins are paid for, and sinners can be forgiven and pardoned.

c. Jesus is the only way to God.

i. Jesus saith unto him, I am the way, the truth, and the life: no man cometh unto the Father, but by me. - Jn 14:6

ii. What separates Christianity from the religions of the world is the sin question: how is our sin forgiven - through our good works or through the Savior Jesus Christ? All religions teach self-effort and self-righteousness, while Christianity teaches the only way to God is through His sinless sacrifice for our sins - His Son, the Lord Jesus Christ, the Savior of the world. All our human attempts to reach God by our own effort will leave us with no guarantee, assurance or peace of mind that we will make it. At best, we can say, "I hope so." But would you want to jump off into eternity with an "I hope so"? Remember, a chance of eternal salvation also means a chance of eternal damnation.

If Jesus is the way, then don't waste your time finding another way - because there is no other way.

10. ALL RELIGIONS ARE THE SAME.

a. If all religions are the same, then why do they teach so differently, and in many places, contradict one another?

    i. The belief of Christianity will exclude all other religions: Jesus saith unto him, I am the way, the truth, and the life: no man cometh unto the Father, but by me. - Jn 14:6

    ii. The belief of Hinduism will embrace practically all kinds of deities.

    iii. The belief of Buddhism denies the existence of a personal, supreme God.

    iv. The belief of Islam will preclude the belief and worship of all the other deities and "isms".

b. All religions may teach us to do good but no one can do good perfectly no matter how much or hard he tries.

    i. Sooner or later, all the religious leaders and their ardent followers will, like Paul, discover to their utter confusion and disillusion, their sincere but futile attempts to be perfectly good - "For that which I do I allow not: for what I would, that do I not; but what I hate, that do I... O wretched man that I am! who shall deliver me from the body of this death?" (Rom 7:15-24)

    ii. The problem is not with the religions but with us - our fallen, sinful and depraved nature can never keep the laws of God or of any religion perfectly. We can suppress our wicked desires for a while but we cannot annihilate them - like a spring, they will bounce back to life again when temptations avail themselves anew to us.

    iii. If we could save ourselves, Jesus would not have had to die for us. We can't and this is why He had to die and pay for the multitude of our sins.

Worst of all my foes, I fear the enemy within. - John Wesley

c. Just as not every kind of medicine can heal a particular life-threatening disease, so, not every religion can save a soul from hell.

    i.   If we, by necessity, must be extremely careful in treating a life-threatening disease, how much more precautions must we take with regard to issues pertaining to our eternal estate.

    ii. We can be wrong with our opinions but we cannot be wrong with our facts.

    iii. If you die wrong the first time you cannot come back to die better a second time. - Robert Murray M'Cheyne

d. Since we have wronged God through our sins, we must come to Him on His terms and conditions.

    i.   **NOT BY OUR RIGHTEOUSNESS:** As it is written, There is none righteous, no, not one. - Rom 3:10

But we are all as an unclean thing, and all our righteousnesses are as filthy rags; and we all do fade as a leaf; and our iniquities, like the wind, have taken us away. - Isa 64:6

Not by works of righteousness which we have done, but according to his mercy he saved us.... - Tit 3:5

    ii. **BUT BY GOD'S RIGHTEOUSNESS:** ... This is the heritage of the servants of the LORD, and their righteousness is of me, saith the LORD. - Isa 54:17

For what saith the scripture? Abraham believed God, and it was counted unto him for righteousness... But to him that worketh not, but believeth on him that justifieth the ungodly, his faith is counted for righteousness. Even as David also describeth the blessedness of the man, unto whom God imputeth righteousness without works. - Rom 4:3-6

Even the righteousness of God which is by faith of Jesus Christ unto all and upon all them that believe: for there is no difference. - Rom 3:22

11. I CANNOT FEEL I NEED TO ACCEPT CHRIST.

a. We make many responsible decisions despite our feelings.

    i. We go to work or school early in the morning even though we may not feel like doing so. This is not hypocrisy but responsibility.

    ii. What would you do if you saw a train coming at you? Would you say, "Let me feel first and then I will move aside," or would you simply step aside because you could see and visualize that you would be killed if you did not do so. Likewise, we do not need to feel first in order to accept the Lord Jesus Christ as our Savior, but we can see that we are in danger of being in hell if we were to die in our sins this very moment.

b. There is seldom any feeling before one dies and is sent to hell.

    i. **DEATH IS SILENT AND SUDDEN:** ... the rich man also died, and was buried; And in hell he lift up his eyes, being in torments... And he cried and said, Father Abraham, have mercy on me, and send Lazarus, that he may dip the tip of his finger in water, and cool my tongue; for I am tormented in this flame. - Lk 16:22-24

    ii. The man who is about to die of a stroke, heart attack or in an auto accident seldom has any feeling to warn him about his impending death. Death, judgment and hell come on padded shoes, quietly and silently, and very often without any sign or warning. This is why we must be prepared for it at all times.

c. Feelings are often unreliable and unpredictable.

    i. There is a way which seemeth right unto a man, but the end thereof are the ways of death. - Prov 14:12

    ii. Better is the sight of the eyes than the wandering of the desire... - Eccl 6:9

Most of our troubles come from following our feelings.

      iii.   "For feelings come, and feelings go. And feelings are deceiving. My warrant is the Word of God. Naught else is worth believing." (William Cowper)

  d.   Those who wait for feelings to decide will decide too late. In hell, there will be a lot of feelings but it will be too late.

      i.   And he cried and said, Father Abraham, have mercy on me, and send Lazarus, that he may dip the tip of his finger in water, and cool my tongue; for I am tormented in this flame. - Lk 16:24

12. I NEED TO SEE A SIGN BEFORE I CAN BELIEVE.

  a.   The sign-seeker errs in his search for God.

      i.   ... Master, we would see a sign from thee. But he (Jesus) answered and said unto them, An evil and adulterous generation seeketh after a sign... - Mt 12:38-39

      ii.   Those whose faith is based on signs will fall with signs - when the signs are not forthcoming. Our faith is based on the unchanging Word of God.

  b.   If we cannot believe the Bible, we will not believe at all - miracle or no miracle.

      i.   ... but if one went unto them from the dead, they will repent. And he (Abraham) said unto him, If they hear not Moses and the prophets, neither will they be persuaded, though one rose from the dead. - Lk 16:27-31

  c.   God has already given us many signs.

      i.   **IN CREATION:** For the invisible things of him from the creation of the world are clearly seen, being understood by the things that are made, even his eternal power and Godhead; so that they are without excuse. - Rom 1:20

      ii.   **IN SCIENCE:** He stretcheth out the north over the empty place, and hangeth the earth upon nothing. - Job 26:7

   iii. **IN PROPHECY:** That then the LORD thy God will turn thy captivity, and have compassion upon thee, and will return and gather thee from all the nations, whither the LORD thy God hath scattered thee. - Deut 30:3

Israel is a living fulfillment of God's prophecy. They were scattered in 70 A.D. and returned in 1948.

13. I AM TOO BUSY - I STILL HAVE TIME TO BELIEVE IN CHRIST.

a. Death is no respecter of age or health. People die in any and every circumstance - in health, in sickness, in old age or in youth. We are all living on borrowed time.

   i. ... The ground of a certain rich man brought forth plentifully: And he thought within himself, saying, What shall I do, because I have no room where to bestow my fruits? And he said, This will I do: I will pull down my barns, and build greater; and there will I bestow all my fruits and my goods. And I will say to my soul, Soul, thou hast much goods laid up for many years; take thine ease, eat, drink, and be merry. **But God said unto him, Thou fool, this night thy soul shall be required of thee: then whose shall those things be, which thou hast provided?** - Lk 12:16-20

   ii. All ages are threatened with death. - Thomas Manton

b. There is only one step between us and death.

   i. ... but truly as the LORD liveth, and as thy soul liveth, there is but a step between me and death. - 1 Sam 20:3

   ii. It takes only a moment for eternity to begin.

c. The real picture of our danger before God.

   i. Let us imagine a submarine that sank into the seabed. Air is running out. A rescue party came and opened the hatch. A voice boomed, "Those who want to be rescued, come up now!" Do you think that the crew inside the

No man is too busy to attend his own funeral.

submarine will say, "Let me think about it, I still have plenty of time to decide, or let me be the first one out?" This is the real picture of our condition before God - we have only the present to decide for Christ and the future may never come. "Too late" is written all over hell.

    ii. **TO THE PHARISEES:** ... O generation of vipers, who hath warned you to flee from the wrath to come? - Mt 3:7

d. We will still have time to believe in Christ provided we know when the time of our death will be. The trouble is, we don't, and the truth is, that time can be any time now.

    i. But God said unto him, Thou fool, this night thy soul shall be required of thee: then whose shall those things be, which thou hast provided? - Lk 12:20

    ii. Those who seek to repent at the eleventh hour usually die at ten-thirty.

e. The things we are often busy about will amount to nothing in the day of our death.

    i. As he came forth of his mother's womb, naked shall he return to go as he came, and shall take nothing of his labour, which he may carry away in his hand. - Eccl 5:15

    ii. Someone once inquired of a relative of a very rich man as to how much he had left behind. "Everything," came the instructive reply. "He took nothing with him."

f. Our priority in life is to be saved first.

    i. For what shall it profit a man, if he shall gain the whole world, and lose his own soul? Or what shall a man give in exchange for his soul? - Mk 8:36-37

    ii. He who provides for this life, but takes no care for eternity, is wise for a moment, but a fool forever. - Tillotson

g. Now is the accepted time to trust in the Lord Jesus Christ. Tomorrow may be too late.

   i. ... behold, now is the accepted time; behold, now is the day of salvation. - 2 Cor 6:2

   ii. You can't repent too soon, because you don't know how soon it may be too late.

   iii. There is nothing more certain than death and nothing more uncertain than the time of death.

14. I HAVE PARENTAL OR FAMILY OBJECTION.

a. If we were to reject Christ because of our family, then we will have no eternal life.

   i. Whosoever therefore shall confess me before men, him will I confess also before my Father which is in heaven. But whosoever shall deny me before men, him will I also deny before my Father which is in heaven... He that loveth father or mother more than me is not worthy of me: and he that loveth son or daughter more than me is not worthy of me. - Mt 10:32-37

   ii. Let us imagine a scenario where a whole family was drowning in a fast-moving river. A lifeline was thrown at them. One of the family members caught the line and said to himself, "Since all of us cannot be saved at the same time, I might as well let go the rope and we all be drowned together." Would it not be better that he got rescued first and then reached out for the rest of his family? Likewise, if he accepts Christ first, then God has a foothold in his family, and they will have a good chance to come to know and believe in Christ - "... Believe on the Lord Jesus Christ, and thou shalt be saved, and thy house." (Acts 16:31)

b. If God has saved us, then He will also be with us to help us through all our difficulties.

   i. **GOD WILL GUIDE US:** I will instruct thee and teach thee in the way which thou shalt go: I will guide thee with mine eye. - Psa 32:8

In courage alone lies safety.

    ii.   **GOD WILL UPHOLD US:** ... for he hath said, I will never leave thee, nor forsake thee. So that we may boldly say, the LORD is my helper, and I will not fear what man shall do unto me. - Heb 13:5-6

c.   We need to relate rightly and wisely with our parents:

    i.   **IN RELATION TO THEIR AUTHORITY:**

Children, obey your parents in all things: for this is well pleasing unto the Lord. - Col 3:20

The boy Jesus was subject to his earthly parents: And when they saw him, they were amazed: and his mother said unto him, Son, why hast thou thus dealt with us? behold, thy father and I have sought thee sorrowing. And he said unto them, How is it that ye sought me? wist ye not that I must be about my Father's business? And they understood not the saying which he spake unto them. And he went down with them, and came to Nazareth, and was subject unto them: but his mother kept all these sayings in her heart. - Lk 2:48-51

Being a Christian does not excuse a child from obeying his parents. In fact, his obedience will help them understand the love and reality of God, and aid their coming to know Christ. His disobedience will be a stumbling block to them.

    ii.   **IN RELATION TO THEIR TRADITION:**

Render therefore to all their dues: tribute to whom tribute is due; custom to whom custom; fear to whom fear; honour to whom honour. - Rom 13:7

Some practices are cultural, customary or just traditional in nature - like the wearing of sackcloth during funerals, the bowing of heads when greeting one another, or the giving of dowries during weddings. However, there are some things in life that are religious or superstitious - the burning of joss sticks to the idols, the prayers to the deceased, or the wearing of charms to protect oneself from harm.

Christians may follow the customs or traditions of their parents or cultures but they are not to follow the devotion and worship of their parents' paganistic gods, religions or superstition.

iii. **IN RELATION TO THEIR RELIGION:**

No man can serve two masters: for either he will hate the one, and love the other; or else he will hold to the one, and despise the other. Ye cannot serve God and mammon. - Mt 6:24

The young Christian is often caught between obeying his parents' wishes and following God; between fearing his parents and honoring God; and agonizes constantly in divided devotion between his parents, who had lovingly and sacrificially raised him up, and the God of his new belief.

The author does not have any simple answer to this very real and agonizing issue but acknowledges the fact that many young Christians, especially in the East, had to go through this process of initial deference to their parents' religions and wishes, and then prayerfully and gradually work towards helping them understand and accept their (the young believers') new-found faith through their testimonies, sharing and stand.

... Behold, now I know that there is no God in all the earth, but in Israel... In this thing the LORD pardon thy servant, that when my master goeth into the house of Rimmon to worship there, and he leaneth on my hand, and I bow myself in the house of Rimmon: when I bow down myself in the house of Rimmon, the LORD pardon thy servant in this thing. And he said unto him, Go in peace. So he departed from him a little way. - 2 Kings 5:15, 18-19

The newly-converted Naaman, under the authority of the paganistic Syrian king, was compelled to bow down himself in the idols' temple. He then sought the forgiveness of God in this matter. The usual

It is only the fear of God that can deliver us from the fear of man.
- John Witherspoon

no-nonsense prophet Elisha, in an understanding and compassionate tone, told him to "go in peace."

This passage shows us that an all-powerful and all-knowing God understands our human circumstances and initial frailty as a young believer. However, He expects us to eventually grow up and take our stand for Him even at the expense of death as in the case of Daniel's three friends: "If it be so, our God whom we serve is able to deliver us from the burning fiery furnace, and he will deliver us out of thine hand, O king. But if not, be it known unto thee, O king, that we will not serve thy gods, nor worship the golden image which thou hast set up." (Dan 3:17-18)

15. **I CANNOT HOLD OUT OR I AM AFRAID I WILL FAIL IF I TRY.**

   a. In reality, no one can live up to the standard of the Bible by himself.

      i. **WE ARE WEAK:** ... the spirit indeed is willing, but the flesh is weak. - Mt 26:41

      ii. **WE ARE WICKED:** The heart is deceitful above all things, and desperately wicked: who can know it? - Jer 17:9

      iii. **WE ARE WAVERING:** For that which I do I allow not: for what I would, that do I not; but what I hate, that do I. - Rom 7:15

   b. It is through the Lord Jesus Christ that we can live by the standard of the Bible.

      i. **HE WILL SAVE US:** Who are kept by the power of God through faith unto salvation ready to be revealed in the last time. - 1 Pet 1:5

      ii. **HE WILL SUCCOR US:** ... but God is faithful, who will not suffer (allow) you to be tempted above that ye are able; but will with the temptation also make a way to escape, that ye may be able to bear it. - 1 Cor 10:13

      iii. **HE WILL STRENGTHEN US:** I can do all things through Christ which strengtheneth me. - Phil 4:13

Look at yourself and your doubts will increase. Look to Jesus and they will disappear. - C. H. Spurgeon

16. THERE IS TOO MUCH TO GIVE UP.

a. There is nothing more important than our souls.

    i. For what shall it profit a man, if he shall gain the whole world, and lose his own soul? - Mk 8:36

b. God loved us enough to give up His Son.

    i. He that spared not his own Son, but delivered him up for us all... - Rom 8:32

    ii. For God so loved the world, that he gave his only begotten Son... - Jn 3:16

c. The things we love in this world will pass away.

    i. Love not the world, neither the things that are in the world. If any man love the world, the love of the Father is not in him. For all that is in the world, the lust of the flesh, and the lust of the eyes, and the pride of life, is not of the Father, but is of the world. And the world passeth away, and the lust thereof: but he that doeth the will of God abideth for ever. - 1 Jn 2:15-17

    ii. To forsake Christ for the world is to leave treasure for a trifle... eternity for a moment, reality for a shadow, all things for nothing. - William Jenkyn

    iii. Life in worldly pleasure is only life in appearance only.

d. What we can get as believers will exceed all that we have given up.

    i. And he said unto them, Verily I say unto you, There is no man that hath left house, or parents, or brethren, or wife, or children, for the kingdom of God's sake, Who shall not receive manifold more in this present time, and in the world to come life everlasting. - Lk 18:29-30

    ii. No man is a fool who gives up what he cannot keep to gain what he cannot lose. - Jim Elliot

    iii. If your treasure is on earth, you are going from it; if it is in heaven, you are going to it.

What shadows we are and what shadows we seek.

17. **THE CHRISTIAN LIFE IS TOO HARD.**

    a. The Christian life is not hard.

        i. **GOD'S WORK IS NOT HARD:** Come unto me, all ye that labour and are heavy laden, and I will give you rest. Take my yoke upon you, and learn of me; for I am meek and lowly in heart: and ye shall find rest unto your souls. For my yoke is easy, and my burden is light. - Mt 11:28-30

        ii. **GOD'S COMMANDMENT IS NOT HARD:** For this is the love of God, that we keep his commandments: and his commandments are not grievous. - 1 Jn 5:3

        iii. All the "thou shalts" and "thou shalt nots" when translated, mean, "Do thyself no harm."

        iv. To obey God is perfect liberty, undisturbed peace and complete rest in our souls. To disobey God is everything otherwise.

    b. The way of sin is harder.

        i. **THE LOST HAS NO EASY LIFE:** ... but the way of the transgressors is hard. - Prov 13:15

        ii. **THE LOST HAS NO ETERNAL LIFE:** For the wages of sin is death... - Rom 6:23 / For what shall it profit a man, if he shall gain the whole world, and lose his own soul? - Mk 8:36

        iii. **THE LOST HAS NO PEACE OF MIND:** But the wicked are like the troubled sea, when it cannot rest, whose waters cast up mire and dirt. There is no peace, saith my God, to the wicked. - Isa 57:20-21

        Even in laughter the heart is sorrowful; and the end of that mirth (merrymaking) is heaviness. - Prov 14:13

    c. In reality, the Christian life is the better life.

        i. **JESUS WANTS TO GIVE US JOY IN OUR SOUL:** These things have I spoken unto you, that my joy might remain in you, and that your joy might be full. - Jn 15:11

It costs much to follow Christ, but it costs more not to.

ii. **JESUS WANTS TO GIVE US PURPOSE IN OUR LIFE:** ... I am come that they might have life, and that they might have it more abundantly. - Jn 10:10

iii. **JESUS WANTS TO GIVE US PEACE IN OUR HEART:** Peace I leave with you, my peace I give unto you: not as the world giveth, give I unto you. Let not your heart be troubled, neither let it be afraid. - Jn 14:27

iv. The lost have no life. They have only an existence.

18. MY HEART IS TOO HARD.

a. God is able to give us a new heart.

   i. A new heart also will I give you, and a new spirit will I put within you: and I will take away the stony heart out of your flesh, and I will give you an heart of flesh. And I will put my spirit within you, and cause you to walk in my statutes, and ye shall keep my judgments, and do them. - Ezek 36:26-27

   ii. Therefore if any man be in Christ, he is a new creature: old things are passed away; behold, all things are become new. - 2 Cor 5:17

   iii. Come now, and let us reason together, saith the LORD: though your sins be as scarlet, they shall be as white as snow; though they be red like crimson, they shall be as wool. - Isa 1:18

b. If we do not repent now, our hearts will get harder. Later on, it will not be a question of whether we will repent or not, but we can't.

   i. But exhort one another daily, while it is called To day; lest any of you be hardened through the deceitfulness of sin. - Heb 3:13

   ii. Can the Ethiopian change his skin, or the leopard his spots? then may ye also do good, that are accustomed to do evil. - Jer 13:23

   iii. Subdue your passion or it will subdue you.

What you are tomorrow, you are becoming today.

19. **I AM TOO GREAT A SINNER.**

    a.   Jesus Christ came into the world to save sinners.

        i.   ... They that be whole need not a physician, but they that are sick... for I am not come to call the righteous, but sinners to repentance. - Mt 9:12-13

        ii.   For the Son of man is come to seek and to save that which was lost. - Lk 19:10

    b.   Paul, before his conversion, was the chief of sinners. Yet, he could be saved.

        i.   This is a faithful saying, and worthy of all acceptation, that Christ Jesus came into the world to save sinners; of whom I am chief. - 1 Tim 1:15

    c.   Jesus Christ turns no one away.

        i.   ... and him that cometh to me I will in no wise cast out. - Jn 6:37

        ii.   God's favorite word is come! - Robert L. Sterner

    d.   The only people who cannot be saved are those who do not want to be saved.

        i.   And ye will not come to me, that ye might have life. - Jn 5:40

20. **I MUST BECOME BETTER BEFORE I CAN BELIEVE IN CHRIST.**

    a.   We go to the doctor when we fall sick. We do not wait to get better before seeing the doctor.

        i.   ... They that be whole need not a physician, but they that are sick... for I am not come to call the righteous, but sinners to repentance. - Mt 9:12-13

        ii.   And the publican, standing afar off, would not lift up so much as his eyes unto heaven, but smote upon his breast, saying, God be merciful to me a sinner. I tell you, this man went down to his house justified rather than the other... - Lk 18:13-14

The Christian message is for those who have done their best and failed.

b. We will never become better before we receive Christ.

    i. For I delight in the law of God after the inward man: But I see another law in my members, warring against the law of my mind, and bringing me into captivity to the law of sin which is in my members. O wretched man that I am! who shall deliver me from the body of this death? I thank God through Jesus Christ our Lord... - Rom 7:22-25

    ii. A sick man will generally get worse without immediate medical care. He does not become better. If we can be perfect and save ourselves, then Jesus did not have to die to save us. The truth is that we can't.

21. WHY DO THE LOST FIND IT HARD TO BELIEVE IN GOD?

a. **BECAUSE OF SIN:** And this is the condemnation, that light is come into the world, and men loved darkness rather than light, because their deeds were evil. - Jn 3:19

    i. Every man, like the moon, has a dark side which no one has seen, and which he hopes no one will ever see - especially God. If God exists, then he is in trouble. This is why he subconsciously suppresses the thought that God might exist - "For every one that doeth evil hateth the light, neither cometh to the light, lest his deeds should be reproved." (Jn 3:20)

    ii. Man will not go to God for the same reason a thief will not go to a policeman.

b. **BECAUSE OF SATAN:** But if our gospel be hid, it is hid to them that are lost: In whom the god of this world hath blinded the minds of them which believe not, lest the light of the glorious gospel of Christ, who is the image of God, should shine unto them. - 2 Cor 4:3-4

    i. I believe Satan exists for two reasons: first, the Bible says so; and second, I've done business with him. - D. L. Moody

I don't swallow the idea that all men are sinners. You don't have to, it is already in you.

c. **BECAUSE OF SELF:** And ye will not come to me, that ye might have life. - Jn 5:40

    i. It is said that there are, in some parts of the world, natives who would use a hollowed coconut or gourd with a hole slightly smaller than the size of the fist of a monkey to catch it. They would fill it with some peanuts, and the monkey, upon seeing the peanuts, would put its hand into it, and grab them. But because its hand was clenched, the monkey could not extract itself from the secured coconut or gourd, thus allowing the natives to catch it. We look at this with much disbelief that these monkeys could be so incredibly foolish enough to lose their lives for just "a few peanuts". But we are just as foolish to lose our souls in hell for all eternity for just "a few peanuts" of worldly enjoyment and sinful pleasures which we cannot let go - "For what shall it profit a man, if he shall gain the whole world, and lose his own soul? Or what shall a man give in exchange for his soul?" (Mk 8:36-37)

    ii. We have to do our own thinking and then we have to do our own dying. Nobody is going to do them for us.

22. HOW ABOUT THOSE WHO HAVE NEVER HEARD OF CHRIST?

a. In the first place, these people are not innocent.

    i. As it is written, There is none righteous, no, not one. - Rom 3:10

    ii. For all have sinned, and come short of the glory of God. - Rom 3:23

b. Also, God's laws are already written in their hearts.

    i. For when the Gentiles (non-Jews), which have not the law, do by nature the things contained in the law, these, having not the law, are a law unto themselves: Which shew (show) the work of the law written in their hearts, their conscience also bearing witness, and their thoughts the mean while accusing or else excusing one another. - Rom 2:14-15

    ii.   Who knowing the judgment of God, that they which commit such things are worthy of death, not only do the same, but have pleasure in them that do them. - Rom 1:32

    iii.   Even when there is no law, there is conscience.

  c.   In addition, God is righteous in judgment.

    i.   He is the Rock, his work is perfect: for all his ways are judgment: a God of truth and without iniquity, just and right is he. - Deut 32:4

    ii.   ... Shall not the Judge of all the earth do right? - Gen 18:25

  d.   Lastly, perhaps God, in His foreknowledge, had already known these people would not believe even if they were presented the gospel.

    i.   ... By hearing ye shall hear, and shall not understand; and seeing ye shall see, and shall not perceive: For this people's heart is waxed gross, and their ears are dull of hearing, and their eyes they have closed; lest at any time they should see with their eyes, and hear with their ears, and should understand with their heart, and should be converted, and I should heal them. - Mt 13:14-15

23. WHO MADE GOD?

  a.   Nobody made God. He is the First Cause and the Uncaused, the Creator of the universe.

    i.   And God said unto Moses, I AM THAT I AM... - Exod 3:14

    ii.   ... I am the first, and I am the last; and beside me there is no God. - Isa 44:6

    iii.   If God did not exist, he would have to be invented. - Voltaire

Conscience doesn't keep you from doing anything; it just keeps you from enjoying it.

b. If there is someone who made God, then by necessity, there must also be a "someone" who made that "someone" who made God. The list would go on and on indefinitely. But no matter how far back we go, there must still be a Self-Existent One by virtue of the visible creation we can see. The truth is that, God is the Self-Existent One, the Creator of all things and the Savior of mankind.

    i. All things were made by him; and without him was not any thing made that was made. - Jn 1:3

    ii. Look unto me, and be ye saved, all the ends of the earth: for I am God, and there is none else. - Isa 45:22

24. I AM A FREETHINKER OR AN ATHEIST.

a. An atheist has no explanation for his existence.

    i. **NO EXPLANATION FOR CREATION:** All things were made by him; and without him was not any thing made that was made. - Jn 1:3

    The Universe is a vacuum. Where then did matter and energy come from? Where did the earth, sun, moon and the constellations of stars come from? Other than God Himself, something cannot come out of nothing. Every effect must have a cause. The energy in the Universe is the effect. What causes it? The Scriptures rightly show the foolishness and inconsistency of man - "The fool hath said in his heart, There is no God..." (Psa 14:1)

    It isn't rational to argue that the world which is based on cause and effect is itself uncaused. - Michael Green

    ii. **NO EXPLANATION FOR INTELLIGENCE:** For the invisible things of him from the creation of the world are clearly seen, being understood by the things that are made, even his eternal power and Godhead; so that they are without excuse. - Rom 1:20

An atheist cannot accept the fact that a car can exist without a maker or a house without a builder. But, at the same time, he can accept the myriad of living things which are millions of times more complex than cars or houses without a Maker or Designer. Where is the logic?

iii. **NO EXPLANATION FOR THE PURPOSE OF LIFE:** Vanity of vanities, saith the Preacher, vanity of vanities; all is vanity. What profit hath a man of all his labour which he taketh under the sun? - Eccl 1:2-3

Why are we here? Where are we going? What is the purpose of life? An atheist has many questions but no real answers.

A truly committed atheist will have to logically believe that he is "from nothing, by nothing, and for nothing".

Atheists are nothing more than bags of molecules banging around until their time is up.

b. An atheist has no excuse in life.

i. **NO EXCUSE FOR NOT KNOWING HIS GOD:** Because that which may be known of God is manifest in them; for God hath shewed it unto them. For the invisible things of him from the creation of the world are clearly seen, being understood by the things that are made, even his eternal power and Godhead; so that they are without excuse. - Rom 1:19-20

ii. **NO EXCUSE FOR NOT KNOWING HIS SINS:** For all have sinned, and come short of the glory of God. - Rom 3:23

iii. **NO EXCUSE FOR NOT KNOWING HIS JUDGMENT:** Who knowing the judgment of God, that they which commit such things are worthy of death, not only do the same, but have pleasure in them that do them. - Rom 1:32

There are more atheists in lip than in life. - Clark H. Pinnock

c.   An atheist has no escape in death.

   i.   **THE SURETY OF JUDGMENT**: And as it is appointed unto men once to die, but after this the judgment. - Heb 9:27

   And I saw the dead, small and great, stand before God; and the books were opened... and the dead were judged out of those things which were written in the books, according to their works. - Rev 20:12

   Be not deceived; God is not mocked: for whatsoever a man soweth, that shall he also reap. For he that soweth to his flesh shall of the flesh reap corruption... - Gal 6:7-8

   ii.   **THE STANDARD OF JUDGMENT**: For all have sinned, and come short of the glory of God. - Rom 3:23

   As it is written, There is none righteous, no, not one. - Rom 3:10

   When we travel to a foreign land, we will be judged by the laws of that land no matter how severe they may be. We cannot demand that we be judged and punished according to our expectations and thinking. Similarly, when we die and meet God, we will be judged by His high and holy standards, and not by our standards, or rather "substandards".

   We are so subnormal that when we try to be normal others will think that we are abnormal.

   iii.   **THE SEVERITY OF JUDGMENT**: And whosoever was not found written in the book of life was cast into the lake of fire. - Rev 20:15

   ... the rich man also died, and was buried; And in hell he lift up his eyes, being in torments... And he cried and said, Father Abraham, have mercy on me, and send Lazarus, that he may dip the tip of his finger in water, and cool my tongue; for I am tormented in this flame. - Lk 16:22-24

You will be a believer some day. If you never believe on earth, you will believe in hell. - Brownlow North

iv. Dr. Jacks tells the story of two friends who had rather blatantly proclaimed themselves to be atheists. When mortal sickness visited one of them, the other came to see him and, perhaps a little afraid lest at the last he should abandon his atheism, said to him, "Stick to it, Bill!" "But," replied the stricken man, "there is nothing to stick to!" - J. D. Jones

25. WHY DO THE WICKED PROSPER AND THE RIGHTEOUS SUFFER?

a. Some of the wicked do prosper and go unpunished.

   i. For I was envious at the foolish, when I saw the prosperity of the wicked... They are not in trouble as other men... Their eyes stand out with fatness: they have more than heart could wish. They are corrupt, and speak wickedly concerning oppression: they speak loftily... Behold, these are the ungodly, who prosper in the world; they increase in riches. - Psa 73:3-12

b. Some of the righteous are bothered by this.

   i. Verily I have cleansed my heart in vain, and washed my hands in innocency. For all the day long have I been plagued, and chastened every morning. If I say, I will speak thus; behold, I should offend against the generation of thy children. When I thought to know this, it was too painful for me. - Psa 73:13-16

c. However, the prosperity of the wicked actually seals their destruction.

   i. Until I went into the sanctuary of God; then understood I their end. Surely thou didst set them in slippery places: thou castedst them down into destruction. How are they brought into desolation, as in a moment! they are utterly consumed with terrors. - Psa 73:17-19

   ii. Sometimes, those whom God wants to destroy, He leaves them alone.

   iii. Who envies the trapped bullock with the ribbons and garlands which decorate him as he is led to the slaughter? - C. H. Spurgeon

God punishes most when He does not punish.

d. The wicked who went unpunished on this side of the grave will be punished on the other side. In death, all wrongs will be made right.

    i. Be not deceived; God is not mocked: for whatsoever a man soweth, that shall he also reap. For he that soweth to his flesh shall of the flesh reap corruption... - Gal 6:7-8

    ii. There was a certain rich man, which was clothed in purple and fine linen, and fared sumptuously every day: And there was a certain beggar named Lazarus, which was laid at his gate, full of sores... And it came to pass, that the beggar died, and was carried by the angels into Abraham's bosom: the rich man also died, and was buried; And in hell he lift up his eyes, being in torments, and seeth Abraham afar off, and Lazarus in his bosom. And he cried and said, Father Abraham, have mercy on me, and send Lazarus, that he may dip the tip of his finger in water, and cool my tongue; for I am torment in this flame. **But Abraham said, Son, remember that thou in thy lifetime receivedst thy good things, and likewise Lazarus evil things: but now he is comforted, and thou art tormented. - Lk 16:19-25**

26. HOW ABOUT THOSE CHRISTIANS WHO ARE HYPOCRITICAL?

a. God will punish a true Christian who sins against Him.

    i. For whom the Lord loveth he chasteneth, and scourgeth every son whom he receiveth. If ye endure chastening, God dealeth with you as with sons; for what son is he whom the father chasteneth not? - Heb 12:6-7

    ii. As many as I love, I rebuke and chasten: be zealous therefore, and repent. - Rev 3:19

b. Some so-called "Christians" are not true Christians.

    i. They profess that they know God: but in works they deny him, being abominable, and disobedient, and unto every good work reprobate. - Tit 1:16

There are hypocrites in the church but there will be no hypocrites in heaven.

ii. He that saith, I know him, and keepeth not his commandments, is a liar, and the truth is not in him. - 1 Jn 2:4

c. These people will be accountable for their sins and we will be accountable to God for our own.

    i. So then every one of us shall give account of himself to God. - Rom 14:12

    ii. And I saw the dead, small and great, stand before God; and the books were opened... and the dead were judged out of those things which were written in the books, according to their works... And whosoever was not found written in the book of life was cast into the lake of fire. - Rev 20:12-15

    iii. The practice of blame-shifting will not work on the day of judgment. We cannot say that we did not believe in Christ because of such people. They will pay for their sins and we will pay for ours.

d. A non-believer tends to be biased or partial in his judgment of Christians.

    i. He will not consistently apply the same rule of judgment to the non-believers - he will not be quick to point out or criticize them when they sin or act hypocritically by virtue of the fact that they do not believe in God. He will not harp on the multitudes of atheists or godless people in prisons today for their horrendous crimes because of their belief in atheism. Neither will he highlight his own sins and inconsistencies as an unbeliever.

    ii. Therefore thou art inexcusable, O man, whosoever thou art that judgest: for wherein thou judgest another, thou condemnest thyself; for thou that judgest doest (do) the same things... And thinkest thou this, O man, that judgest them which do such things, and doest the same, that thou shalt escape the judgment of God? - Rom 2:1-3

If you are looking for another hypocrite, just look into the mirror - you will find one more.

27. WHY ARE THERE SO MANY DENOMINATIONS?

a. This is due to the failures of man and not of God.

i. **BECAUSE OF OUR IGNORANCE - WE DO NOT KNOW:** And a certain Jew named Apollos, born at Alexandria, an eloquent man, and mighty in the scriptures, came to Ephesus. This man was instructed in the way of the Lord; and being fervent in the spirit, he spake and taught diligently the things of the Lord, knowing only the baptism of John. And he began to speak boldly in the synagogue: whom when Aquila and Priscilla had heard, they took him unto them, and expounded unto him the way of God more perfectly. - Acts 18:24-26

ii. **BECAUSE OF OUR INCOMPETENCY - WE DO NOT STUDY:** Study to shew thyself approved unto God, a workman that needeth not to be ashamed, rightly dividing the word of truth. - 2 Tim 2:15

iii. **BECAUSE OF OUR IDEOLOGY - WE DO NOT CHANGE WHEN WE ARE WRONG:** Beloved, believe not every spirit, but try the spirits whether they are of God: because many false prophets are gone out into the world. - 1 Jn 4:1

We can either study the Bible with our minds made up or we can study the Bible to make up our minds.

b. Satan will do his best to discredit Christianity and to divide Christians.

i. Lest Satan should get an advantage of us: for we are not ignorant of his devices. - 2 Cor 2:11

ii. If we have the capability to counterfeit a particular currency, which currency would we choose? We would probably choose the US dollars, or some other valuable currency rather than some worthless monies to counterfeit. Satan, too, knows that Christianity is the only way to God, and he seeks to divide and confuse Christians as much as possible.

c. However, most evangelical denominations have essentially the same fundamentals.

   i. Most evangelicals may have differences on some important issues but they are in agreement on many of the fundamentals of the faith - Salvation by Faith in Jesus Christ, the Blood Atonement of Christ, Eternal Security, the Verbal and Plenary Inspiration of the Bible, the belief in the Trinity, Special Creationism, the Literal Second Coming of Christ, etc.

d. Interestingly, the multiplicity of denominations also reveals the love and tolerance in Christendom among the evangelicals.

   i. Although many evangelicals may not necessarily work with one another at the church level, yet there is a common love and respect for each other as the children of God.

   ii. ... That ye love one another; as I have loved you, that ye also love one another. By this shall all men know that ye are my disciples, if ye have love one to another. - Jn 13:34-35

28. WHY ARE CHRISTIANS CONSTANTLY BOTHERING OTHERS ABOUT THEIR FAITH?

a. It is a Christian's duty to warn others about their coming judgment.

   i. Ask him what would he do if he saw a blind man walking towards a cliff or a neighbor's home on fire? Should he walk away and turn a blind eye or would it not be his duty to warn them about the impending dangers? Likewise, every Christian has the responsibility to warn others about the coming judgment of God.

   ii. Knowing therefore the terror of the Lord, we persuade men... - 2 Cor 5:11

It is impossible to save a life from burning and avoid the heat of the fire. - Mary S. Wood

iii. When I say unto the wicked, Thou shalt surely die; and thou givest him not warning, nor speakest to warn the wicked from his wicked way, to save his life; the same wicked man shall die in his iniquity; but his blood will I require at thine hand. - Ezek 3:18

iv. When Christians evangelize, they are not engaging in some harmless and pleasant pastime. They are engaging in a fearful struggle, the issues of which are eternal. - Leon Morris

b. It is out of love and concern that a Christian shares his faith with others.

i. Open rebuke is better than secret love. - Prov 27:5

ii. Whenever a believer shares his faith, he stands to be misunderstood, embarrassed and ridiculed, a price he is willing to pay to see a soul saved - "... though the more abundantly I love you, the less I be loved." (2 Cor 12:15)

29. WHAT HAPPENS TO BABIES AND LITTLE CHILDREN WHO DIED?

a. As far as the clear Scriptures have shown, these little ones will be in heaven.

i. But now he is dead, wherefore should I fast? can I bring him back again? I shall go to him but he shall not return to me. - 2 Sam 12:23

King David will one day go and meet his dead child but his dead child cannot come back to him in his lifetime. This shows that the child is in heaven as David is a saved man.

ii. But Jesus said, Suffer (allow) little children, and forbid them not, to come unto me: for of such is the kingdom of heaven. - Mt 19:14

b. However, there is an age of accountability in which the child will be answerable for his sins. This varies from child to child.

All things are not necessarily good but all things work together for good to them that love God.

71

i. And should not I spare Nineveh, that great city, wherein are more than sixscore (120) thousand persons that cannot discern between their right hand and their left hand (these are children); and also much cattle? - Jonah 4:11

ii. If these little children cannot tell their right hand from their left hand how then can they be accountable for their sins? However, there will come a day when they will be answerable for their sins.

c. Sometimes, God, in allowing these little ones to die, may want to spare them from unnecessary or unbearable suffering to come.

i. ... and when thy feet enter into the city, the child shall die. And all Israel shall mourn for him, and bury him: for he only of Jeroboam shall come to the grave, because in him there is found some good thing toward the LORD God of Israel in the house of Jeroboam. - 1 Kings 14:12-13

ii. "Where was God when my son died?" asked a distraught mother. "The same place when His Son died on the cross," came the wise reply.

30. WHY DOES GOD ALLOW SATAN, SIN AND SUFFERING TO EXIST?

a. God did create a perfect environment twice, and on both occasions, the independent beings (Satan and Man) He created failed miserably.

i. **THE PERFECTION AND PRIDE OF SATAN:**

Thou wast perfect in thy ways from the day that thou wast created, till iniquity was found in thee. - Ezek 28:15

For thou hast said in thine heart, I will ascend into heaven, I will exalt my throne above the stars of God: I will sit also upon the mount of the congregation, in the sides of the north: I will ascend above the heights of the clouds; I will be like the most High. - Isa 14:13-14

In the resurrection morning... we shall thank God for every storm.
- J. C. Ryle

ii. **THE COMPLETION AND CONDEMNATION OF MAN:**

So God created man in his own image, in the image of God created he him; male and female created he them. - Gen 1:27

And when the woman saw that the tree was good for food, and that it was pleasant to the eyes, and a tree to be desired to make one wise, she took of the fruit thereof, and did eat, and gave also unto her husband with her; and he did eat. - Gen 3:6

b. God did not create independent beings like us to be robots without a free will or choice, but rather He gave us the liberty to choose - either for Him or against Him.

    i. ... choose you this day whom ye will serve... - Josh 24:15

    ii. And ye will not come to me, that ye might have life. - Jn 5:40

c. One day, all these things will pass away.

    i. **SIN WILL BE REMOVED:** As far as the east is from the west, so far hath he removed our transgressions from us. - Psa 103:12

    ii. **SATAN WILL BE DESTROYED:** And the devil that deceived them was cast into the lake of fire and brimstone... and shall be tormented day and night for ever and ever. - Rev 20:10

    iii. **SUFFERING WILL BE HISTORY:** And God shall wipe away all tears from their eyes; and there shall be no more death, neither sorrow, nor crying, neither shall there be any more pain: for the former things are passed away. - Rev 21:4

d. God allows all these things to test and reward us (the believers) for our obedience.

    i. **TO PROVE US:** And thou shalt remember all the way which the LORD thy God led thee these forty years in the wilderness, to humble thee, and to prove thee, to know what was in thine heart, whether thou wouldest keep his commandments, or no. - Deut 8:2

The whole of life is a test, a trial of what is in us, so arranged by God himself. - William S. Plumer

ii. **TO PERFECT US:** But the God of all grace, who hath called us unto his eternal glory by Christ Jesus, after that ye have suffered a while, make you perfect, stablish, strengthen, settle you. - 1 Pet 5:10

Knowing this, that the trying of your faith worketh patience. But let patience have her perfect work, that ye may be perfect and entire, wanting (lacking) nothing. - Jas 1:3-4

God is not in the habit of changing our circumstances but of changing us.

The gem cannot be polished without friction, nor can man be perfected without trials.

iii. **TO PREPARE US:** For I reckon that the sufferings of this present time are not worthy to be compared with the glory which shall be revealed in us. - Rom 8:18

For our light affliction, which is but for a moment, worketh for us a far more exceeding and eternal weight of glory. - 2 Cor 4:17

But lay up for yourselves treasures in heaven, where neither moth nor rust doth corrupt, and where thieves do not break through nor steal: For where your treasure is, there will your heart be also. - Mt 6:20-21

Over the triple doorways of the Cathedral of Milan there are three inscriptions spanning the splendid arches. Over one is carved a beautiful wreath of roses, and underneath is the legend, "All that pleases is but for a moment." Over the other is sculptured a cross, and these are the words beneath: "All that troubles is but for a moment." But underneath the great central entrance in the main aisle is the inscription, "That only is important which is eternal."

The hiding places of men are discovered by affliction.

31. I HAVE TRIED CHRISTIANITY AND FAILED.

   a. **SOME ARE DISILLUSIONED:**

      i. For it was not an enemy that reproached me; then I could have borne it: neither was it he that hated me that did magnify himself against me; then I would have hid myself from him: But it was thou, a man mine equal, my guide, and mine acquaintance. We took sweet counsel together, and walked unto the house of God in company. - Psa 55:12-14

      ii. Some Christians are so disillusioned with other Christians whom they trusted and respected, that they doubt God, quit church and backslide.

   b. **SOME ARE DISCOURAGED:**

      i. For the good that I would I do not: but the evil which I would not, that I do... For I delight in the law of God after the inward man: But I see another law in my members, warring against the law of my mind, and bringing me into captivity to the law of sin which is in my members. O wretched man that I am! who shall deliver me from the body of this death? - Rom 7:19-24

      ii. Some truly born-again Christians are so discouraged by their own sins and failures, that they are sure that they are not saved or can never be saved. These believers usually are not grounded in the Word of God and are unable to overcome the temptations of the world through the power of God.

   c. **SOME ARE DECEIVED (SELF-DECEIVED):**

      i. But it is happened unto them according to the true proverb, The dog is turned to his own vomit again; and the sow that was washed to her wallowing in the mire. - 2 Pet 2:22

        If we are not truly converted or saved, then like the pig that is washed which will head back to the mud again, we too, will find excuses about not obeying God and go back to our old, sinful ways.

Practice does not make perfect; it is perfect practice that makes perfect. - Vince Lombardi

ii.   I was once speaking to a woman who had been a professed Christian but had given it all up. I asked her why she was not a Christian any longer? She replied that she did not believe the Bible. I asked her why she did not believe the Bible. "Because I have tried its promises and found them untrue." "Which promises?" "The promises about prayer?" "Which promises about prayer?" "Does it not say in the Bible, 'Whatsoever ye ask believing ye shall receive?'" "It says something like that." "Well, I asked fully expecting to get and did not receive, so the promise failed." "Was the promise made to you?" "Why, certainly, it is made to all Christians, is it not?" "No, God carefully defines who the ye's are whose believing prayers He agrees to answer." I then turned her to 1 John 3:22 (And whatsoever we ask, we receive of him, because we keep his commandments, and do those things that are pleasing in his sight.), and read the description of those whose prayers had power with God. "Now," I said, "were you keeping His commandments and doing those things which are pleasing in His sight?" She frankly confessed that she was not, and she soon came to see that the real difficulty was not with God's promises, but with herself. That is the reason for many unanswered prayers today: the one who offers them is not obedient. - R. A. Torrey

iii. Some people "believed in Christ" for the wrong reasons - for wealth, health or a good life. They have little interest in following or obeying God. To them, God is like: a Santa Claus to provide them with regular gifts, or an aspirin for their occasional headaches, or a lawyer when they needed one. No wonder they are disappointed when things did not turn out the way they expected. They are like the "house built on sand" waiting for the storms to come and destroy it.

God being who he is must always be sought for himself, never as a means towards something else. - A. W. Tozer

d. These people should re-examine themselves as to whether they have come to know God in the right way.

    i. Were they trusting in God alone or looking to man for their spiritual guidance and growth? Man may fail us but not God - the best of man, is still man, at best.

    ii. Were they regular in church and taught systematically the Word of God? A believer who is not grounded in the Bible is easily tossed to and fro by life's problems and beset by personal sins.

    iii. Were they sincerely seeking God on His terms and conditions or just deceiving themselves? Do they love the Giver (God) or the gifts?

32. **WHY SHOULD THE WICKED, WHO REPENTED AT THE LAST MOMENT, GO TO HEAVEN, WHILE THE RIGHTEOUS, WHO REFUSED TO ACCEPT JESUS CHRIST END UP IN HELL?**

a. In the first place, there is no such thing as a righteous man. He may be righteous relative to other people, but he is not righteous in an absolute sense before a Holy God.

    i. As it is written, There is none righteous, no, not one. - Rom 3:10

    ii. For all have sinned, and come short of the glory of God. - Rom 3:23

    iii. There are no moral men; only moral sinners or immoral sinners.

    iv. We are all like a box of rotten apples - some are more rotten than others. There is none good or perfect.

b. God did save the sincere, dying thief on the cross.

    i. **THE THIEF ON THE CROSS:** And one of the malefactors which were hanged railed on him, saying, If thou be Christ, save thyself and us. But the other answering rebuked him, saying, Dost not thou fear God, seeing thou art in the same condemnation? And we indeed justly; for we receive the due reward of our deeds: but

Christ's vicarious death was deficient for none; sufficient for all; and efficient only for those who believe.

this man hath done nothing amiss. And he said unto Jesus, Lord, remember me when thou comest into thy kingdom. And Jesus said unto him, Verily I say unto thee, To day shalt thou be with me in paradise. - Lk 23:39-43

c. However, God will not save anyone who schemes to cheat on Him.

   i. A story was related somewhat like this: A Christian was inquiring of an unbeliever as to why he did not want to accept Jesus Christ immediately. The answer was, "I want to be like the dying thief who accepted Christ in his final moment. In the meantime, I want to enjoy the worldly pleasures this life can afford me." The Christian's reply was, "He was a dying thief who sincerely repented and was saved. But you are a living thief who is bent on cheating God."

   ii. God, who is all-knowing, sees the heart. He knows how to differentiate between an insincere and a sincere seeker - "... for the Lord seeth not as man seeth; for man looketh on the outward appearance, but the LORD looketh on the heart." (1 Sam 16:7) Even Judas Iscariot, who was an apostle, preacher, baptizer and miracle-worker, could not deceive God - he died tragically a lost man in the end.

d. Ironically, the most difficult people to be saved are the self-righteous who think they are too good to end up in Hell.

   i. The Pharisee stood and prayed thus with himself, God, I thank thee, that I am not as other men are, extortioners, unjust, adulterers, or even as this publican. I fast twice in the week, I give tithes of all that I possess... for every one that exalteth himself shall be abased; and he that humbleth himself shall be exalted. - Lk 18:11-14

   ii. ... Verily I say unto you, That the publicans and the harlots go into the kingdom of God before you (the self-righteous Pharisees). - Mt 21:31

Late repentance is seldom true, but true repentance is never too late.

iii. It is said that a doctor once gave similar medication to two patients suffering from TB (Tuberculosis). One lived while the other died. The staff of the hospital were puzzled until they found out the patient who died had hid his medicine under his pillow and did not take it. God too, offers pardon to all - the wicked and the "righteous". If the so-called "righteous" refused and ended up in Hell, while the wicked accepted Christ and lived eternally in Heaven, then the "righteous" will have themselves to be blamed eventually.

33. SINCE A CHRISTIAN'S SINS HAVE BEEN PAID FOR - PAST, PRESENT AND FUTURE - DOES THAT MEAN HE CAN CONTINUE IN SINS?

a. A true believer will not take advantage of the forgiveness and pardon of God.

    i. What shall we say then? Shall we continue in sin, that grace may abound? God forbid. How shall we, that are dead to sin, live any longer therein? - Rom 6:1-2

    ii. What then? shall we sin, because we are not under the law, but under grace? God forbid. - Rom 6:15

b. Our obedience or good works, or the lack of them, will reveal who we really are. In the final analysis, we will do according to what we truly believe in.

Even so every good tree bringeth forth good fruit; but a corrupt tree bringeth forth evil fruit. A good tree cannot bring forth evil fruit, neither can a corrupt tree bring forth good fruit. - Mt 7:17-18

    i. <u>A genuine, living faith will cause one to fear God and depart from evil.</u>

Was not Abraham our father justified by works, when he had offered Isaac his son upon the altar? Seest thou how faith wrought (work) with his works, and by works was faith made perfect? - Jas 2:21-22

... I will shew thee my faith by my works. - Jas 2:18

Nowhere does the Bible tell us that salvation is by a faith that does not work. - R. B. Kuiper

ii. <u>An insincere, dead faith will cause one to continue unrepentantly in sins.</u>

He that saith, I know him, and keepeth not his commandments, is a liar, and the truth is not in him.
- 1 Jn 2:4

Thou believest that there is one God; thou doest well: the devils also believe, and tremble. But wilt thou know, O vain man, that faith without works is dead?
- Jas 2:19-20

Know ye not, that to whom ye yield yourselves servants to obey, his servants ye are to whom ye obey; whether of sin unto death, or of obedience unto righteousness?
- Rom 6:16

c. God, who is our Heavenly Father, will discipline or chastise His children when they sin against Him.

i. For whom the Lord loveth he chasteneth, and scourgeth every son whom he receiveth. If ye endure chastening, God dealeth with you as with sons; for what son is he whom the father chasteneth not? - Heb 12:6-7

ii. The heavenly Father has no spoiled children. He loves them too much to allow that. - Fred Mitchell

d. Those who would willfully take advantage of God's pardon and continue in sins are likely to be lost.

i. Know ye not that the unrighteous shall not inherit the kingdom of God? Be not deceived: neither fornicators, nor idolaters, nor adulterers, nor effeminate, nor abusers of themselves with mankind, Nor thieves, nor covetous, nor drunkards, nor revilers, nor extortioners, shall inherit the kingdom of God. And such were some of you: but ye are washed, but ye are sanctified, but ye are justified in the name of the Lord Jesus, and by the Spirit of our God. - 1 Cor 6:9-11

ii. ... whosoever doeth not righteousness is not of God, neither he that loveth not his brother. - 1 Jn 3:10

The lost leap into sin and love it; the saved lapse into sin and loathe it.

34. WHY DOES PAUL TEACH SALVATION BY FAITH WHILE JAMES SEEMS TO TEACH SALVATION BY WORK?

a.   Paul shows us the basis of our salvation - we are saved by depending on our faith in the Lord Jesus Christ and not on our good works.

    i.   For by grace are ye saved through faith; and that not of yourselves: it is the gift of God: Not of works, lest any man should boast. - Eph 2:8-9

    ii.   And if by grace, then is it no more of works: otherwise grace is no more grace. But if it be of works, then is it no more grace: otherwise work is no more work. - Rom 11:6

    iii.   For therein is the righteousness of God revealed from faith to faith: as it is written, The just shall live by faith. - Rom 1:17

b.   James, on the other hand, shows us the quality of that faith - it is a living, vibrant, genuine and sincere faith that will cause one to do the works of the Bible, and not a dead faith that will cause one to pay lip service to God and do nothing.

    i.   **A DEAD FAITH:** What doth it profit, my brethren, though a man say he hath faith, and have not works? can faith save him? If a brother or sister be naked, and destitute of daily food, And one of you say unto them, Depart in peace, be ye warmed and filled; notwithstanding ye give them not those things which are needful to the body; what doth it profit? Even so faith, if it hath not works, is dead, being alone. - Jas 2:14-17

    ii.   **A LIVING FAITH:** Was not Abraham our father justified by works, when he had offered Isaac his son upon the altar? Seest thou how faith wrought (work) with his works, and by works was faith made perfect? And the scripture was fulfilled which saith, Abraham believed God, and it was imputed unto him for righteousness:

and he was called the Friend of God. Ye see then how that by works a man is justified, and not by faith (that is, a dead faith) only. - Jas 2:21-24

iii. It is said that Charles Blondin, a world renown tightrope walker, once asked a journalist if he believed that he (Blondin) would be able to walk across the Niagara Falls on the tightrope. The jouralist's instant reply was, "Yes." Then said the tightrope walker, "Climb on my back and I will carry you over." "No way," came the nervous reply. The journalist had a "dead faith" - he believed in his head but not in his heart.

35. WHAT ABOUT THE BELIEFS OF KARMA, REBIRTH, NIRVANA, ETC?

a. The basis of these beliefs.

i. Some Eastern religions and philosophies hold on to the belief that life is a process of birth, death and rebirth in which one's station in life depends on one's karma or the works he has done in his past life. If he has done well, then his next life will be good and vice versa. The ultimate goal is to escape rebirth through enlightenment and good deeds, and reach Nirvana which is to be absorbed back into the universe.

b. The fallacies of these beliefs.

i. First, the end result of rebirth and reincarnation is to pay for all our sins or to have a zero account with regard to our sins. In short, to be pure or "sinless". But in the first place, when we first entered into the world, logically we had to be "sinless" because we had not committed any sins yet. That being the case, why then did we come into this world to experience birth, suffering, death and rebirth? Why then did the process of birth and rebirth begin?

ii. Secondly, why would an all-powerful and all-knowing God require so many births and rebirths to know who we are? God, because of His foreknowledge, knows

Human philosophy is the art of learning more and more about less and less until we know everything about nothing.

who we are or what we will be like even before we are actually born. Our birth and existence is more for ourselves than for God - we will stand before Him inexcusable on the day of judgment. We cannot say that we were not given a chance to prove ourselves.

... I am God, and there is none like me. Declaring the end from the beginning, and from ancient times the things that are not yet done, saying, My counsel shall stand, and I will do all my pleasure. - Isa 46:9-10

iii. Thirdly, life's suffering is not the result of bad past karma but rather in accordance to the foreknowledge and purpose of God. Some people are born blind, deaf or retarded, not because of some bad, past karma but because God may want to restrain them from their destructive potential or He may use such handicaps to help these people come to know Him. Don't we wish that men like Adolph Hitler who gassed six million Jews in the Holocaust during World War II were born blind or deaf?

TO RESTRAIN MAN: And lest I should be exalted above measure through the abundance of the revelations, there was given to me a thorn in the flesh, the messenger of Satan to buffet me, lest I should be exalted above measure. - 2 Cor 12:7

TO REVEAL GOD: ... Master, who did sin, this man, or his parents, that he was born blind? Jesus answered, Neither hath this man sinned, nor his parents: but that the works of God should be made manifest in him. - Jn 9:1-3

iv. Fourthly, the Bible teaches eternal judgment rather than rebirth. If the Bible is true in its prophecies and science, then it will be true also with regard to the eternal estate of man.

... the rich man also died, and was buried; And in hell he lift up his eyes being in torments... And he cried and said, Father Abraham, have mercy on me, and send Lazarus, that he may dip the tip of his finger in water, and cool my tongue; for I am tormented in this flame. - Lk 16:22-24

And whosoever was not found written in the book of life was cast into the lake of fire. - Rev 20:15

v. <u>Fifthly, practices like being a vegetarian, very often associated with these beliefs, are found to be inconsistent.</u>

If vegetarians are honest and objective enough, they will realize that plants and vegetables are not "lifeless" but are just another form of life. In short, they are still killing lives, albeit a different form of life. Also, it has been scientifically proven that plants and vegetables, when attacked, do send out some kind of distress signals.

Forbidding to marry, and commanding to abstain from meats, which God hath created to be received with thanksgiving of them which believe and know the truth. For every creature of God is good, and nothing to be refused, if it be received with thanksgiving. - 1 Tim 4:3-4

36. CAN GOD MAKE A STONE SO HEAVY THAT HE CANNOT CARRY IT?

This is a common trick question put forth by the atheists to trap a Christian. The logic of the argument is this: If God **can** make a stone so heavy that he cannot carry it, then he is not all-powerful, because he "cannot carry it". If God **cannot** make a stone so heavy that he cannot carry it, then he is again not all-powerful, because he "cannot do it". Either way, God is shown to be not all-powerful, and if He is not omnipotent, then He is not God, and therefore God does not exist.

a. We need to differentiate between an "impossible situation" and an "impossible task".

i. An "impossible situation" is one that cannot exist in real life. For example, there is no such thing as a "square circle" or a "round square", or a "bright darkness" or a "dark light".

In the case of an "impossible situation", you can delete "God" out of the equation and subsitute with another "person" into it - can an all-powerful "Buddha" or "Allah" make a stone so heavy the he cannot carry it? And it still cannot be done because it is an "impossible situation" (one cannot be all-powerful whether one can or cannot make a stone so heavy that one cannot carry it).

This trick question is not about the "who" - who can or cannot do it; but it is about the "what" - it creates an impossible situation that just cannot exist in reality, like a square circle, and then unfairly challenge somebody to make it happen. Nobody can make what cannot possibly exist to happen!

Another equally silly question is this: "Can a man make a spear so strong that it can pierce any shield and, at the same time, make a shield so tough that no spear can pierce it?" This scenario does not exist and therefore nobody can do it, and there is no apology needed to explain why it cannot be done!

ii.   An "impossible task", on the other hand, is something humanly impossible to man, but possible to God because He is an all-powerful God.

The Universe is a vacuum or nothingness, and an all-powerful God can and did create all the matter and energy in the Universe out of nothing - a task which is totally impossible with man but is ridiculously easy with God. He literally speaks the world into existence - "In the beginning God created the heaven and the earth. And the earth was without form, and void; and darkness was upon the face of the deep... And God said, Let there be light: and there was light." (Gen 1:1-3)

Behold, I am the LORD, the God of all flesh: is there any thing too hard for me? - Jer 32:27

For with God nothing shall be impossible. - Lk 1:37

b.   Even if there are some things that God cannot do, it does not disprove His existence. In fact, we should be thankful that there are some things God cannot do.

i. **GOD CANNOT LIE:** In hope of eternal life, which God, that cannot lie, promised before the world began. - Tit 1:2

ii. **GOD CANNOT SIN:** To shew that the LORD is upright: he is my rock, and there is no unrighteousness in him. - Ps 92:15

iii. **GOD CANNOT BE TEMPTED WITH EVIL:** Let no man say when he is tempted, I am tempted of God: for God cannot be tempted with evil, neither tempteth he any man. - Jas 1:13

c. This is a classic example of the extent fallen mankind will go to to deny the obvious existence of an Almighty God. God is knowable through His Creation, and yet man chooses to willfully deny His existence by his foolishness.

i. **GOD REVEALS:** For the invisible things of him from the creation of the world are clearly seen, being understood by the things that are made, even his eternal power and Godhead; so that they are without excuse. - Rom 1:20

ii. **MAN REJECTS:** Because that, when they knew God, they glorified him not as God, neither were thankful; but became vain in their imaginations, and their foolish heart was darkened. Professing themselves to be wise, they became fools. - Rom 1:21-22

iii. **HEAVEN RIDICULES:** Why do the heathen rage, and the people imagine a vain thing? The kings of the earth set themselves, and the rulers take counsel together, against the LORD... He that sitteth in the heavens shall laugh: the Lord shall have them in derision. - Psa 2:1-4

iv. If God the Creator did not exist, then the creation which we see and man's very own existence are a lie. "All things were made by him; and without him was not any thing made that was made." (Jn 1:3)

Where there is no God there is no man. - Nicolai Berdyaeu

37. **WHAT ABOUT ASTROLOGY, NECROMANCY, PARANORMAL ACTIVITIES, UFOS, EXTRATERRESTRIAL BEINGS, ETC?**

   a.   The potential of Satan.

       i.   **SATAN CAN PERFORM MIRACLES:** For there shall arise false Christs, and false prophets, and shall shew great signs and wonders; insomuch that, if it were possible, they shall deceive the very elect. - Mt 24:24

            The elect will not be deceived and the deceived will not be the elect.

            For they are the spirits of devils, working miracles, which go forth unto the kings of the earth and of the whole world... - Rev 16:14

            One of the characteristics of the end times will be the proliferation of demonic miracles and deceptions.

            If there arise among you a prophet, or a dreamer of dreams, and giveth thee a sign or a wonder, And the sign or wonder come to pass, whereof he spake unto thee, saying, Let us go after other gods, which thou hast not known, and let us serve them; Thou shalt not hearken unto the words of that prophet, or that dreamer of dreams: for the LORD your God proveth you, to know whether ye love the LORD your God with all your heart and with all your soul. - Deut 13:1-3

       ii.   **SATAN CAN PRETEND TO BE GOOD:** For such are false apostles, deceitful workers, transforming themselves into the apostles of Christ. And no marvel; for Satan himself is transformed into an angel of light. Therefore it is no great thing if his ministers also be transformed as the ministers of righteousness; whose end shall be according to their works. - 2 Cor 11:13-15

            Now the Spirit speaketh expressly, that in the latter times some shall depart from the faith, giving heed to seducing spirits, and doctrines of devils... Forbidding to marry, and commanding to abstain from meats, which God hath created to be received with thanksgiving of them which believe and know the truth. - 1 Tim 4:1-3

Satan does not mind that we be religious as long as we do not have the Savior - the Lord Jesus Christ.

iii. **SATAN CAN POSSESS HUMAN BEINGS:** And certain women, which had been healed of evil spirits and infirmities, Mary called Magdalene, out of whom went seven devils. - Lk 8:2

Then entered Satan into Judas surnamed Iscariot, being of the number of the twelve. - Lk 22:3

b. The purpose of Satan.

i. **SATAN SEEKS TO BLIND:** But if our gospel be hid, it is hid to them that are lost: In whom the god of this world hath blinded the minds of them which believe not, lest the light of the glorious gospel of Christ, who is the image of God, should shine unto them. - 2 Cor 4:3-4

ii. **SATAN SEEKS TO DECEIVE:** Even him, whose coming is after the working of Satan with all power and signs and lying wonders. - 2 Thess 2:9

iii. **SATAN SEEKS TO DESTROY:** Be sober, be vigilant; because your adversary the devil, as a roaring lion, walketh about, seeking whom he may devour. - 1 Pet 5:8

iv. Satan promises the best, but pays the worst; he promises honor and pays with disgrace; he promises pleasure and pays with pain; he promises profit and pays with loss; he promises life and pays with death. - Thomas Brooks

c. The possibility of Satan.

i. **ASTROLOGY:** Thou art wearied in the multitude of thy counsels. Let now the astrologers, the stargazers, the monthly prognosticators, stand up, and save thee from these things that shall come upon thee (the coming Babylonian invasion of Israel). - Isa 47:13

ii. **WITCHCRAFT:** And I will cut off witchcrafts out of thine hand; and thou shall have no more soothsayers. - Mich 5:12

iii. **NECROMANCY:** Regard not them that have familiar spirits, neither seek after wizards, to be defiled by them: I am the LORD your God. - Lev 19:31

Satan is mighty but he is not Almighty.

38. **WHERE DOES THE BIBLE SHOW THAT JESUS CHRIST IS GOD?**

   a. **HIS DIVINE ATTRIBUTES.**

       i. **HE IS ETERNAL:** ... whose goings forth have been from of old, from everlasting. - Mich 5:2

      ii. **HE IS OMNIPRESENT (ALL-PRESENT):** And no man hath ascended up to heaven, but he that came down from heaven, even the Son of man which is in heaven. - Jn 3:13

     iii. **HE IS OMNISCIENT (ALL-KNOWING):** ... of Christ. In whom are hid all the treasures of wisdom and knowledge. - Col 2:2-3

     iv. **HE IS OMNIPOTENT (ALL-POWERFUL)**: All things were made by him; and without him was not any thing made that was made. - Jn 1:3

   b. **HIS DIVINE TITLES.**

       i. **GOD:** In the beginning was the Word, and the Word was with God, and the Word was God. - Jn 1:1

The New World Translation of the Jehovah Witnesses would translate this verse as "a god" instead of "God" because they claim that there is no article "the" before the word "God". However, in the Greek, Jn 1:6,12,13 & 18 also do not have the article "the" before the word "God", and yet they are translated as "God" and not "a god" in the NWT.

And Thomas answered and said unto him, My Lord and my God. Jesus saith unto him, Thomas, because thou hast seen me, thou hast believed: blessed are they that have not seen, and yet have believed. - Jn 20:28-29

Looking for that blessed hope, and the glorious appearing of the great God and our Saviour Jesus Christ. - Tit 2:13

The Son of God became the Son of Man in order that the sons of men might become the sons of God.

According to the Granville Sharp Rule, when the copulative "kai" (and) connects two nouns of the same case, if the article precedes the first noun and is not repeated before the second noun, the latter always refers to the same person that is expressed or described by the first noun. In short, "the great God and our Saviour Jesus Christ" here are one and the same Person.

But unto the Son he saith, Thy throne, O God, is for ever and ever: a sceptre of righteousness is the sceptre of thy kingdom. - Heb 1:8

And without controversy great is the mystery of godliness: God was manifest in the flesh... - 1 Tim 3:16

ii. **THE SON OF GOD:** The Jews answered him, We have a law, and by our law he ought to die, because he made himself the Son of God. - Jn 19:7

But Jesus answered them, My Father worketh hitherto (until now), and I work. Therefore the Jews sought the more to kill him, because he not only had broken the sabbath, but said also that God was his Father, making himself equal with God. - Jn 5:17-18

To the Jews, the Son of God is also God, the Son - "For unto us a child is born, unto us a son is given: and the government shall be upon his shoulder: and his name shall be called Wonderful, Counsellor, The mighty God, The everlasting Father..." (Isa 9:6)

iii. **THE MIGHTY GOD:** For unto us a child is born, unto us a son is given: and the government shall be upon his shoulder: and his name shall be called Wonderful, Counsellor, The mighty God, The everlasting Father, The Prince of Peace. - Isa 9:6

Jehovah is also called the mighty God: "The remnant shall return, even the remnant of Jacob, unto the mighty God." (Isa 10:21) See also Jer 32:18 & Psa 50:1

God had only one Son, and He was a missionary. - David Livingstone

iv. **THE ALMIGHTY GOD: Behold, he cometh with clouds;** and every eye shall see him, and they also which pierced him: and all kindreds of the earth shall wail because of him. Even so, Amen. **I am Alpha and Omega,** the beginning and the ending, saith the Lord, which is, and which was, and which is to come, **the Almighty.** - Rev 1:7-8

And, behold, I come quickly; and my reward is with me, to give every man according as his work shall be. **I am Alpha and Omega,** the beginning and the end, the first and the last... He which testifieth these things saith, Surely I come quickly. Amen. **Even so, come, Lord Jesus.** - Rev 22:12-20

The 'Alpha and Omega' in Rev 22:12-20, who is the Lord Jesus Christ, is the same as the 'Alpha and Omega' of Rev 1:7-8, which is the Almighty God. Besides, there is no such thing as the Second Coming of the Father.

v. **THE FIRSTBORN:** Who is the image of the invisible God, the firstborn (prototokos) of every creature. - Col 1:15

The Greek word used is "prototokos" (firstborn) and not "protoktistos" (first-created). Here, "firstborn" is used to denote the position of pre-eminence or supremacy of the Lord Jesus Christ - "For by him were all things created, that are in heaven, and that are in earth, visible and invisible... all things were created by him, and for him: And he is before all things, and by him all things consist... that in all things he might have the preeminence." (Col 1:16-18)

Israel is called God's firstborn although it was not the first nation to exist - "And thou shalt say unto Pharaoh, Thus saith the LORD, Israel is my son, even my firstborn." (Exod 4:22) Ephraim is known as Jehovah's firstborn - "... for I am a father to Israel, and Ephraim is my firstborn." (Jer 31:9) This is in spite of the fact that Mannaseh is the biological firstborn of Joseph - "... Ephraim... who was the younger... for Manasseh was the firstborn." (Gen 48:13-14)

vi. **THE BEGOTTEN:** I will declare the decree: the LORD hath said unto me, Thou art my Son; this day have I begotten thee. - Psa 2:7 / Heb 1:5

The Scriptures uses this phrase 'this day have I begotten thee' in the context of Christ's ressurection and not in the sense that He was 'created': "God hath fulfilled the same unto us their children, in that he hath raised up Jesus again; as it is also written in the second psalm, Thou art my Son, this day have I begotten thee." (Acts 13:33)

vii. **THE ONLY BEGOTTEN:** For God so loved the world, that he gave his only begotten (monogenes) Son... - Jn 3:16

The Greek word "monogenes" with reference to the Lord Jesus Christ means "only one of its kind, unique." (Vine's Expository Dictionary of New Testament Words; Thayer's Greek-English Lexicon)

Isaac was called the "only begotten" son of Abraham - "By faith Abraham, when he was tried, offered up Isaac... his only begotten son." (Heb 11:17) In reality, Abraham had other children - Ishmael, who was the biological firstborn of Abraham (Gen 16:1-16) and the other children of his concubines (Gen 25:1-6).

viii. **THE BEGINNING OF THE CREATION OF GOD:** ... These things saith the Amen, the faithful and true witness, the beginning of the creation of God. - Rev 3:14

The word "beginning" (arche) can be translated as "source" or "active cause" as in Rev 1:8 - "I am Alpha and Omega, the beginning (arche) and the ending, saith the Lord, which is, and which was, and which is to come, the Almighty." God, who is the Almighty, has no "beginning" but He is the "Source" of all creation.

c. **HIS DIVINE ASSOCIATION:**

i. **I and my Father are one...** The Jews answered him,

I have a great need for Christ; I have a great Christ for my need.
- C. H. Spurgeon

saying, For a good work we stone thee not; but for blasphemy; and because that thou, being a man, makest thyself God. - Jn 10:30-33

The Lord Jesus went on to stress on His divinity by:

EQUATING HIMSELF WITH JEHOVAH IN THE PSALMS: Jesus answered them, Is it not written in your law, I said, Ye are gods? - Jn 10:34

I (with reference to Jehovah) have said, Ye are gods; and all of you are children of the most High. But ye shall die like men... - Psa 82:6-7

Here the 'gods' refer to human judges (not the Mormon's "gods") - "God standeth in the congregation of the mighty; he judgeth among the gods. How long will ye judge unjustly, and accept the persons of the wicked? Selah." (Psa 82:1-2)

USING HIS DIVINE TITLE 'THE SON OF GOD': Say ye of him, whom the Father hath sanctified, and sent into the world, Thou blasphemest; because I said, I am the Son of God? - Jn 10:36

RE-EMPHASIZING HIS CORRELATION WITH THE FATHER: ... that the Father is in me, and I in him. - Jn 10:38

ii.　... Christ Jesus: Who, being in the form of God, thought it not robbery to be equal with God. - Phil 2:5-6

d.　**HIS DIVINE WORSHIP:**

i.　And again, when he bringeth in the first begotten into the world, he saith, And let all the angels of God worship him. - Heb 1:6

The footnote in the New World Translation (Large Print 1971 edition) states that "obeisance" is also translated as "worship".

e. **HIS DIVINE CONDESCENSION:**

i. When the Lord Jesus Christ came into this world to die for our sins, He "emptied Himself" in order to take on the nature of man and die in our place. For this reason, He could be hungry, thirsty and eventually "taste death for every man" (Heb 2:9).

Let this mind be in you, which was also in Christ Jesus: Who, being in the form of God, thought it not robbery to be equal with God: But made himself of no reputation, and took upon him the form of a servant, and was made in the likeness of men: And being found in fashion as a man, he humbled himself, and became obedient unto death, even the death of the cross. - Phil 2:5-8

ii. With this self-imposed, limited exercise of His prerogative, we can understand the following passages:

He did not know the exact time of His Second Coming: But of that day and that hour knoweth no man, no, not the angels which are in heaven, neither the Son, but the Father. - Mk 13:32

He depended completely on His Father: Then answered Jesus and said unto them, Verily, verily, I say unto you, The Son can do nothing of himself, but what he seeth the Father do: for what things soever he doeth, these also doeth the Son likewise. - Jn 5:19

iii. In the functioning of the Godhead (nature of God):

JESUS CHRIST IS EQUAL TO THE FATHER IN PERSON: Let this mind be in you, which was also in Christ Jesus: Who, being in the form of God, thought it not robbery to be equal with God. - Phil 2:5-6

JESUS CHRIST IS SUBORDINATED TO THE FATHER IN POSITION: ... that the head of every man is Christ; and the head of the woman is the man; and the head of Christ is God. - 1 Cor 11:3

He who made man was made man.

... for my Father is greater than I (that is, in position but not in person). - Jn 14:28

The Lord Jesus Christ is equal with the Father in person but is subordinated to Him in position just as the woman is equal to the man in person but is subordinated to him in position. This subordination has nothing to do with Christ's essence or nature - He is God. In a similar way, the woman, being in subordination, is not inferior to the man in the sense of being 'subhuman' in nature.

39. **WHAT ABOUT THE TRINITY - ONE GOD EXISTING IN THREE DISTINCT PERSONS?**

   a.   The Bible teaches that there is only one God.

      i.   Hear, O Israel, The LORD our God is one LORD. - Deut 6:4

      ii.   ... we know... that there is none other God but one. - 1 Cor 8:4

      iii.   ... before me there was no God formed, neither shall there be after me. I, even I, am the LORD; and beside me there is no saviour. - Isa 43:10-11

      This contradicts the teaching of the "plurality of gods" as taught by the Mormons - God was never a man and man can never be God.

   b.   The Bible also teaches that there are three distinct Persons in the Godhead (nature of God).

      i.   **The Father is God**: ...Grace to you, and peace, from God our Father... - Rom 1:7

      ii.   **The Son is God:** But unto the Son he saith, Thy throne, O God, is for ever and ever: a sceptre of righteousness is the sceptre of thy kingdom. - Heb 1:8

      iii.   **The Holy Spirit is God:** But Peter said, Ananias, why hath Satan filled thine heart to lie to the Holy Ghost... thou hast not lied unto men, but unto God. - Acts 5:3-4

c. The Bible also points to the existence of the Trinity.

    i. **In the plural name for God (Elohim):** In the beginning God (Elohim) created the heaven and the earth. - Gen 1:1

       God standeth in the congregation of the mighty; he judgeth among the gods (elohim). - Psa 82:1

    ii. **In the plural forms of the personal pronouns of God:** And God said, Let **us** make man in **our** image, after **our** likeness. - Gen 1:26 / Gen 11:7 / Isa 6:8

    iii. **In the Theophanies** (the appearances of God in a human form): And the angel of the LORD called unto him out of heaven, and said, Abraham, Abraham: and he said, Here am I. And he said, Lay not thine hand upon the lad... for now I know that thou fearest God, seeing thou hast not withheld thy son, thine only son from me. - Gen 22:11-12 / Gen 31:11-13 / Exod 3:1-15

    iv. **In the Baptismal Formula:** Go ye therefore, and teach all nations, baptizing them **in the name (singular)** of the Father, and of the Son, and of the Holy Ghost. - Mt 28:19

    v. **In the "Thrice Holy" proclamation by the seraphims (angelic beings):** And one cried unto another, and said, **Holy, holy, holy,** is the Lord of hosts: the whole earth is full of his glory. - Isa 6:3

    vi. **In the oneness of the three Witnesses:** For there are three that bear record in heaven, the Father, the Word, and the Holy Ghost: and these three are one. - 1 Jn 5:7

       Some have doubted the veracity of this verse but there are ample proofs:

       6 MSS (61, 88mg, 429, 629, 636mg and 918) contain this verse. In addition, 2 lectionaries (60, 173) and 4 church fathers quoted it - Tertullian (160-230 A.D.),

The word "Trinity' is not found in the Bible, but the truth of this doctrine is in every part of it. - Donald Grey Barnhouse

Cyprian (200-258 A.D.), Augustine (354-430 A.D.) and Jerome (340-420 A.D.). This is on top of the fact the Vulgate (2nd - 4th century), the early Latin translation of the Greek Manuscripts, has it. In all probability, Origen, the well-known corrupter of his days was responsible in the deletion of this verse from the majority of the Greek manuscripts.

d. Nature also hints at the existence of the Trinity.

   i.   Time has past, present and future.

   ii. Matter has length, breadth and height.

   iii. Water can exist as solid, liquid or gas.

e. God, if He chooses to, can exist as three distinct Persons and yet be one God.

   i.   **GOD IS NOT ABOVE HIS MORAL LAWS:**

        Thou art of purer eyes than to behold evil, and canst not look on iniquity... - Hab 1:13

        For thou art not a God that hath pleasure in wickedness: neither shall evil dwell with thee. - Psa 5:4

        God cannot sin in an absolute sense.

   ii. **HOWEVER, GOD IS ABOVE HIS PHYSICAL AND NUMERICAL LAWS:**

        He could part the Red Sea, perform miracles, raise the dead, multiply the loaves of bread, etc.

        God, who is Sovereign and Omnipotent (all-powerful), can do what He will and nothing is impossible to Him. We, because of our finite minds and human limitations, will never fully comprehend an infinite God. If God chooses to exist in three distinct Persons, who are we to impose on Him that He can't, just because we cannot understand it? In existing as a Triune Being, He has not violated any of His moral laws.

In addition, God, because of His attribute of Omni-presence (being all-present), can easily exist in three different Persons and yet remain as One God.

It is said that Augustine, one of the early church fathers, was once troubled by the concept of the Trinity. While walking along the beach, he chanced upon a boy emptying buckets of water into a hole in the sand. "What are you doing boy?" he asked. "Trying to empty the ocean into this hole," came the childish answer. It then dawn upon Augustine that he too, in trying to comprehend the Trinity, was trying to "empty the ocean into a hole", that is, trying to comprehend an infinite God with his finite mind.

40. HOW ABOUT EVOLUTION?

a. In reality, life, with its complexities, cannot come from inorganic matter without any external intelligence or help.

   i. Can plaster, timber and nails, when left on their own, organize themselves into a house or an apartment? Can an explosion in a printing shop result in an unabridged dictionary being produced? They can't and neither can the complexity of life evolve from inorganic matter by itself without an external intelligence, no matter how long the time element may be.

   ii. Every living thing is made up of trillions of living cells. The simplest living cell consists of millions of parts put together simultaneously without which it cannot live. All our technology and know-how today cannot even create "a fraction of a fraction" of a living cell.

   iii. Each cell has a DNA which is the genetic code of the species. It is estimated that there is enough information in each DNA to fill up 1,000 volumes of the Encyclopedia Britannica. Every creature has its own DNA. The DNA will determine what species it will be, how it will grow and develop, when the parts will be formed, what parts each cell will produce and what parts it will not, etc. Can such highly complex DNA exist through the process of chance or accident? No, it can't!

Our narrow thoughts can no more comprehend the Trinity in Unity than a nutshell will hold all the water in the sea. - Thomas Watson

iv. The Second Law of Thermodynamics, simply stated, teaches that all things, living or non-living, are heading towards disorderliness rather than to something more organized or complex. If we were to leave an apple or a dead animal alone, it would rot and decompose. It would not evolve into something more complex. Likewise, if we let alone a car or a house for a long time, it will rust and break down.

b. One species cannot evolve into another.

i. There are variations (micro-evolution) - crossbreeding of dogs or cats will produce different kinds of dogs or cats; but cats do not evolve into dogs (macro-evolution).

ii. The DNA of each species actually fixes the species and determines whether it is a dog, cat or plant. Changes in the DNA are known as mutations. 99.7 to 99.9 percent of all mutations are harmful. Babies born with defective or faulty livers, lungs or hearts seldom live long. The remaining percentage of mutations are either neutral or duplicative (an extra finger, toe, etc). The commonly propounded theory of the "survival of the fittest" is, in reality, the "preservation of the species" - the strongest and fittest of the species survive within the bounds of their original, God-created DNA. They do not evolve into another species.

"Do we, therefore, ever see mutations going about the business of producing new structures for selection to work on? No nascent organ has ever been observed emerging... Neither observation nor controlled experiment has shown natural selection manipulating mutations so as to produce a new gene, hormone, enzyme system or organ." (Michael Pitman, Adam and Evolution, London: Rider, 1984, pp. 67–68)

"It is a striking, but not much mentioned fact that, though geneticists have been breeding fruit-flies for sixty years or more in labs all round the world—flies which produce a new generation every eleven days— they have never yet seen the emergence of a new

Those who believe in evolution are going to make a monkey out of themselves.

99

species or even a new enzyme." (Gordon Rattray Taylor (former Chief Science Advisor, BBC Television), The Great Evolution Mystery, New York: Harper & Row, 1983, p. 48)

iii. Fossil records fly in the face of the evolutionists as they do not show any of the millions of missing links supposedly to have existed between the species. The problem with the missing links is that they are still missing. Fossil records simply show that all these species existed just as they do today. It is just that some of these species have become extinct.

iv. Microbiologists realize that the genetic gaps between species are just too great for evolution. It is like a man trying to do a long jump, a mile long, over the Grand Canyon in one go. He cannot do it in a series of jumps. Similarly, for one species to "evolve" into another, it must achieve it with one transformation or it will not survive. No fish will become a land animal with a series of changes. It must change its gills into fully developed lungs in one move or it will die on land. It cannot have half-developed or "semi-evolved" lungs and still survive.

v. If evolution is true, then we will still be witnessing life being formed from inorganic matter or some creatures still in the evolutionary process. We can't see any of them today in spite of the tens of thousands of varieties of species around us.

c. The fallacy of the "Geologic Column."

i. In the realm of nature, the neatly-drawn, textbook version of the complete Geologic Column of the fossil records does not exist. Poly-strata fossils, missing layers, layers out of order, misplaced fossils, and layers in reverse order, all invalidate the geologic column. For example, all over the world, undisturbed sedimentary layers of the more complex fossils have been found beneath those with the simple ones, proving that the theory of the simpler forms of life evolving into the more complex ones is not true. Worst still, fossilized trees have been found to cut through several strata of fossils showing that all these fossils were deposited at the same time and not over "millions of years." Likewise, footprints of dinosaurs and man have been found together on the Paluxy River bed near Glen Rose, Texas, USA, disproving the theory that man and dinosaurs were separated by millions of years.

ii. There is circular reasoning in the dating of the age of fossils and their corresponding rock strata. The geologist dates the age of the rocks by the fossils found in them, and then in turn, the evolutionist dates the age of the fossils by the rocks identified with them.

"The intelligent layman has long suspected circular reasoning in the use of rocks to date fossils and fossils to date rocks. The geologist has never bothered to think of a good reply, feeling the explanations are not worth the trouble as long as the work brings results." (J. E. O'Rourke, American Journal of Science, 1976, 276:51)

d. Also, to be able to accurately date a specimen by radiometric means, the following must be known:

i. The original amount of the parent isotopes at the beginning of the specimen existence.

ii. The amount of daughter isotopes or the absence of them in the beginning.

iii. There must be no addition or subtraction of the parent or daughter isotopes thereafter.

iv. The rate of decay from the parent to daughter isotopes is constant.

v. None of these can be known for sure and this explains why various samples of the same specimen will give different dates.

If evolution is true, then my Volkswagen will turn into a Cadillac in about ten years' time.

vi. "The troubles of the radiocarbon dating method are undeniably deep and serious. Despite 35 years of technological refinement and better understanding, the underlying assumptions have been strongly challenged, and warnings are out that radiocarbon may soon find itself in a crisis situation. Continuing use of the method depends on a "fix it as we go" approach, allowing for contamination here, fractionation there, and calibration whenever possible. It should be no surprise, then, that fully half of the dates are rejected. The wonder is, surely, that the remaining half come to be accepted. No matter how 'useful' it is, though, the radiocarbon method is still not capable of yielding accurate and reliable results. There are gross discrepancies, the chronology is uneven and relative, **and the accepted dates are actually selected dates.**" (Lee, Robert. "Radiocarbon, Ages in Error," Anthropological Journal of Canada, Vol. 19, No. 3, 1981, pp 9,29)

vi. "It may come as a shock to some, but fewer than 50 percent of the radiocarbon dates from geological and archaeological samples...have been adopted as "acceptable" by investigators." (J. Ogden III, Annals of the New York Academy of Science, Vol 288, 1977, pg 167-173)

e. Creationism is more credible than Evolution.

i. In the beginning God created the heaven and the earth. - Gen 1:1

ii. All things were made by him; and without him was not anything made that was made. - Jn 1:3

iii. If all the living things in the world which are so highly complex cannot exist by chance, then the only logical explanation left is that an intelligent Creator has made them just as they are today. It is like looking at a radio or a computer and realizing that they cannot exist by chance, and thus logically concluding that an intelligent being must have made them. The obvious alternative to chance is an intelligent Designer. In addition, all living and non-living things in the world have a "symbiotic relationship" - they

The question is not whether man descended from the monkey, but when is he going to stop descending?

complement and need one another in order to make life possible. If there were no sunlight or oxygen or water or ozone layer, life would have been impossible. If all the parts in a cell did not exist simultaneously or all the vital organs of a man were not present at the same time, life would have been impossible. All this shows the existence and reality of God behind His creation. Evolution demands progression and progression demands that there was at one time, a semi-developed heart, lung, liver, or an imperfect and incomplete immune, digestive or reproductive system. But we know that no living animal will survive for a moment with half a heart, kidney or any of its vital organs. Either they come complete or they die. It is not that an atheist cannot believe in God, it is that he won't. It is not an intellectual problem, it is a heart problem. As the Bible says, "For the invisible things of him from the creation of the world are clearly seen, being understood by the things that are made, even his eternal power and Godhead; so that they are without excuse. Because that, when they knew God, they glorified him not as God, neither were thankful; but became vain in their imaginations, and their foolish heart was darkened. Professing themselves to be wise, they became fools." (Rom 1:20-22)

iv. "Scientists who go about teaching that evolution is a fact of life are great con-men, and the story they are telling may be the greatest hoax ever. In explaining evolution, we do not have one iota of fact." (Dr T. N. Tahmisian, Atomic Energy Commission, USA)

v. "Evolution is unproved and unprovable. We believe it because the only alternative is special creation which is unthinkable." (Sir Arthur Keith, British evolutionist) The fool hath said in his heart, There is no God... - Psa 14:1

vi. "Scripture answers three basic questions to which the evolutionary theory has no answer whatsoever. These questions concern the origin of matter, the origin of life and the origin of man as a religious being." (R. B. Kuiper)

f.   Scientific evidences against Evolution.

i.   **DIVINE CREATION:**

Amino acids in living things are all left-handed. Half of the amino acids in non-living things are right-handed and the other half are left-handed. There is no known natural process that can isolate either the left-handed or right-handed variety.

Proteins consist of amino acids and amino acids cannot join together in the presence of oxygen. If there is oxygen, the first protein cannot be formed. If there is no oxygen, there will be no ozone in the upper atmosphere. And if there is no ozone, all living things will be killed by the ultraviolet rays from the sun.

Richard E. Dickerson, "Chemical Evolution and the Origin of Life," Scientific American, Vol. 239, September 1978:

·   "The amino acids must link together to form proteins, and the other chemicals must join up to make nucleic acids, including the vital DNA. The seemingly insurmountable obstacle is the way the two reactions are inseparably linked - one can't happen without the other. Proteins depend on DNA for their formation. But DNA cannot form without pre-existing protein." Hitching, p. 66.

"Genes and enzymes are linked together in a living cell - two interlocked systems, each supporting the other. It is difficult to see how either could manage alone. Yet if we are to avoid invoking either a Creator or a very large improbability, we must accept that one occurred before the other in the origin of life. But which one was it? We are left with the ancient riddle: Which came first, the chicken or the egg?" Shapiro, p. 135.

What men fear is not that death is annihilation but that it is not. - Epicurus

ii. **FOSSIL RECORDS:**

WE KNEW BETTER: "And it has been the paleontologist – my own breed - who have been most responsible for letting ideas dominate reality... We paleontologist have said that the history of life supports that interpretation [gradual adaptive change], all the while knowing that it does not." (Niles Eldredge, Columbia U., American Museum Of Natural History, TIME FRAMES, 1986, p.144)

PRESENCE OF 'GAPS': "Despite the bright promise that paleontology provides a means of 'seeing' evolution, it has presented some nasty difficulties for evolutionists the most notorious of which is the presence of 'gaps' in the fossil record. Evolution requires intermediate forms between species and paleontology does not provide them." (David B. Kitts, an evolutionist and paleontologist, Major Features of Evolution, 28:467)

120 YEARS AFTER DARWIN: "We are now about 120 years after Darwin and the knowledge of the fossil record has been greatly expanded. We now have a quarter of a million fossil species but the situation hasn't changed much - ironically, we have even fewer examples of evolutionary transition than we had in Darwin's time. By this I mean that some of the classic cases of Darwinian change in the fossil record such as the evolution of the horse in North America, have had to be discarded or modified as a result of more detailed information." (David M. Raup, Univ. Chicago; Chicago Field Mus. of N. H. Field, Bulletin, 50:22-29)

"TREES" NOT FROM FOSSILS: "The evolutionary trees that adorn our textbooks have data only at the tips and nodes of their branches; the rest is inference, however reasonable, not the evidence of the fossils." (Steven J. Gould, Harvard, Natural History, V. 86, p.13)

FOSSILS IN AN ADVANCED STATE OF EVOLUTION: "And we find many of them already in an advanced state of evolution, the very first time they appear. It is as though they were just planted there, without any evolutionary history. Needless to say, this appearance of sudden planting has delighted creationists... the only alternative explanation of the sudden appearance of so many complex animal types in the Cambrian era is divine creation..." (Richard Dawkins, Cambridge, THE BLIND WATCHMAKER, 1986, pg 229-230)

iii. **IRREDUCIBLE COMPLEXITY:**

THE COMPLEXITY OF LIVING CELLS: Each component of a living cell is breathtakingly complex, yet in isolation it cannot survive nor replicate itself. All the parts of the cell are necessary to its functioning and replication. Nothing works until everything works. This has been called irreducible complexity. Even small parts of the components of cells can be unimaginably complex. An example of this is the enzyme adenosine triphosphate synthase, found in all living cells including animals, plants, fungi and bacteria. The elucidation of the structure of ATP synthase won a 1997 Nobel Prize. Every cell contains hundreds of these miniature motors embedded in the surfaces of the mitochondria. Each is 200,000 times smaller than a pinhead. The motor forges a bond between ADP and phosphate to form ATP. The ATP couples with other processes in the cell requiring energy to reform ADP and phosphate. So energy is directed to contract muscles, beat the heart and drive thought processes in the brain, while the products are recycled. At the centre of ATP synthase is a tiny wheel that turns at about 100 revolutions per second and turns out three ATP molecules per rotation. Just to keep us thinking and walking, humans must recycle their own body weight of ATP each day. Each enzyme is composed of thirty-one separate proteins that in turn are made of thousands of precisely arranged amino acids. Take away any one of the 31 proteins and the motor is useless. It could not have evolved. And consider this: the genetic information and RNA plus proteins needed to construct the ATP synthase are in total even

Surely the best of men are but men at best. - Thomas Brooks

more irreducibly complex than the ATP synthase itself. A car-making factory is more complex than a car." (David Rosevear, The Myth of Chemical Evolution)

THE COMPLEXITY OF THE HUMAN EYE: The eye, as one of the most complex organs, has been the symbol and archetype of his (Darwin's) dilemma. Since the eye is obviously of no use at all except in its final, complete form, how could natural selection have functioned in those initial stages of its evolution when the variations had no possible survival value? No single variation, indeed no single part, being of any use without every other, and natural selection presuming no knowledge of the ultimate end or purpose of the organ, the criterion of utility, or survival, would seem to be irrelevant. And there are other equally provoking examples of organs and processes which seem to defy natural selection. Biochemistry provides the case of chemical synthesis built up in several stages, of which the intermediate substance formed at any one stage is of no value at all, and only the end product, the final elaborate and delicate machinery, is useful - and not only useful but vital to life. How can selection, knowing nothing of the end or final purpose of this process, function when the only test is precisely that end or final purpose? - Gertrude Himmelfarb, Darwin and the Darwinian Revolution (Garden City, New York: Doubleday, 1959, pp. 320-321)

"While today's digital hardware is extremely impressive, it is clear that the human retina's real-time performance goes unchallenged. Actually, to simulate 10 milliseconds (one hundredth of a second) of the complete processing of even a single nerve cell from the retina would require the solution of about 500 simultaneous nonlinear differential equations 100 times and would take at least several minutes of processing time on a Cray supercomputer. Keeping in mind that there are 10 million or more such cells interacting with each other in complex ways, it would take a minimum of 100 years of Cray time to simulate what takes place in your eye many times every second." (John Stevens, Byte magazine, April 1985)

THE COMPLEXITY OF THE E. COLI BACTERIUM: A bacterium commonly found in our intestinal tract, Escherichia coli, is a sausage-shaped cell about 1/10,000th of an inch long. Each microbe is fitted with five or six long, flexible flagella with which it propels itself through the fluid medium. Until about 1972 it was thought that the flagella undulated or wiggled. Then it was found that they actually rotate! This startling discovery initiated intense research which has elucidated

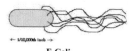

← 1/10,000th inch →

E Coli

some amazing facts about the propulsion system of E. coli. The flagella are not entirely flexible but have the form of a corkscrew or helical propeller. Each flagellum connects by a universal joint to the shaft of the motor. This shaft protrudes from the side of the bacterium, and since its flagellum must trail behind, the universal joint is needed to transmit the rotary motion around a right angle. On the inner end of the shaft is the rotor of the motor. The shaft passes through two disks fixed in the bacterial wall. The first is the stator of the motor. The second, outer disk serves as a sleeve bearing. Figure 1 is an engineering sketch of this amazing micro-mechanism. The motor is a constant torque, variable speed, reversible rotary motor! It is also an electric motor, energized by a flow of positively charged protons through the cell membrane. The sensory and control system is also complex and sophisticated.

Can evolutionary theory explain the origin of this propulsion system? Dr. Robert Macnab, at the close of a fifty-page review article admitted it could not. Prof. Howard Berg of the California Institute of Technology, a leading authority on the subject, could not in a private conversation provide an explanation. In fact, Darwin's own theory predicts that such a complex combination of complex, interdependent parts could not evolve. This is because if any of the parts

To be an atheist, one would have to believe that what is made exists, but that which made it does not. - M. R. Kopmeyer

began to evolve, they would be a costly, useless burden to the organism. Any microbes which began to evolve the system would have to expend energy and building materials to produce something useless. They would not be able to compete with the unchanged microbes around them and therefore would be eliminated from the population by natural selection. Thus evolution would be stopped in its tracks.

The rotary motor of E. coli. The rotor is attached rigidly to the inner end of the shaft, the outer end of which connects to the hook (a universal joint) which attaches to the inner end of the flagellar filament. The stator and the bearing are fixed rigidly to the inner and outer membranes of the cell. The rotor, hook and flagellum rotate at approximately 100 revolutions per second. (Adapted from Bruce Alberts et al., Molecular Biology of the Cell (Garland Publishing, New York, 1983), p. 758, by Bible-Science News, Vol. 32, 1994, No. 2, p. 11)

In view of all these facts and more, it is not "unscientific" in the least to believe that E. coli was designed and created by God.

"Darwin complained his critics did not understand him, but he did not seem to realize that almost everybody, friends, supporters and critics, agreed on one point, his natural selection cannot account for the origin of the variations, only for their possible survival. And the reasons for rejecting Darwin's proposal were many, but first of all that many innovations cannot possibly come into existence through accumulation of many small steps, and even if they can, natural selection cannot accomplish it, because incipient and intermediate stages are not advantageous." (Søren Løvtrup, Darwinism: The Refutation of a Myth, New York: Croom Helm, 1987, pp. 274–275)

Charles Darwin wrote: "If it could be demonstrated that any complex organ existed which could not possibly have been formed by numerous successive, slight modifications, my theory would absolutely break down." (Charles Darwin, Origin of Species)

iv. **THE DIFFERENT SEXES:**

We know that simple forms of life reproduce by "mitosis", a process in which the cell divides itself into two identical cells. What causes two "globs of cells" to suddenly want to change their ways of reproduction - where one says, "I will change to a "male" and you will change to a "female"?

For such a process to occur, both parties must "evolve" simultaneously, completely and independently with such precision that the anatomical, chemical, and electrical systems of their reproductive organs complement each other. If any party "misses a step", the species goes straight into extinction. We have to keep in mind the vast complexity of the millions of independent parts and systems involved at the molecular level in the "sperms" and "eggs", the reproductive organs, and the cognitive and emotional functioning of the species in order to draw them together. Also, just out of curiosity, where did they get the blueprints for the different and yet complementary reproductive organs? In addition, this "independent evolution" into the male and female of a species must be repeated millions of times for all the other existing creatures and plants.

Faith in God who created all things male and female would probably be more acceptable and credible than such mind-boggling improbability - "But from the beginning of the creation God made them male and female." (Mk 10:6)

He that knows nothing will believe anything. - Thomas Fuller

Reproduction is essential for the continuity and survival of any species. The obvious question is: how is it possible for the species to reproduce when their reproductive organs are still in the process of evolving?

For more information, please search the internet for:

Answers in Genesis
Institute for Creation Research
Creation Science Institute

Fossilized Tree cutting through the different strata of rocks.

Taylor's Trail of footprints of dinosaur and man criss-crossing each other.

Courtesy of R. Patton and www.bible.ca

THE PRECEPT IN PERSONAL EVANGELISM

1. **A SCRIPTURAL MESSAGE**

   a. **THE RIGHT GOSPEL:** Moreover, brethren, I declare unto you the gospel which I preached unto you, which also ye have received, and wherein ye stand; By which also ye are saved, if ye keep in memory what I preached unto you, unless ye have believed in vain. For I delivered unto you first of all that which I also received, how that Christ died for our sins according to the scriptures; And that he was buried, and that he rose again the third day according to the scriptures. - 1 Cor 15:1-4

      i. The true Gospel consists of the finished work of our Lord Jesus Christ - His death, burial and resurrection; and the complete payment of our sins, both past, present and future.

   b. **THE WRONG GOSPEL:** I marvel that ye are so soon removed from him that called you into the grace of Christ unto another gospel: Which is not another, but there be some that trouble you, and would pervert the gospel of Christ. But though we, or an angel from heaven, preach any other gospel unto you than that which we have preached unto you, let him be accursed. As we said before, so say I now again, If any man preach any other gospel unto you than that ye have received, let him be accursed. - Gal 1:6-9

      i. Anything, no matter how good or noble it may be, when added to the Gospel of our Lord Jesus Christ, becomes "another gospel" which cannot save us. It is like adding a little poison to a good portion of wholesome food. Some unfortunately would add baptism, sacraments, sabbath-keeping, tongues-speaking, law-keeping, good works, evangelistic fervor, et al., to the Gospel thus making it of no effect to the believers.

      ii. Nothing needs to be added to Christ's finished work, and nothing can be added to Christ's finished work. - Francis Schaeffer

Do not believe the devil's gospel, which is a chance of salvation: a chance of salvation is a chance of damnation. - Adolph Saphir

iii. If our gospel be wrong, then we will end up like the Pharisees whom Jesus condemned - "Woe unto you, scribes and Pharisees, hypocrites! for ye compass sea and land to make one proselyte, and when he is made, ye make him twofold more the child of hell than yourselves." - Mt 23:15

2. A SCRIPTURAL MESSIAH

a. **THE RIGHT MESSIAH:** When Jesus came into the coasts of Caesarea Philippi, he asked his disciples, saying, Whom do men say that I the Son of man am? And they said, Some say that thou art John the Baptist: some, Elias; and others, Jeremias, or one of the prophets. He saith unto them, But whom say ye that I am? And Simon Peter answered and said, Thou art the Christ, the Son of the living God. And Jesus answered and said unto him, Blessed art thou, Simon Bar-jona: for flesh and blood hath not revealed it unto thee, but my Father which is in heaven. - Mt 16:13-17

   i. Peter's concept of our Lord Jesus Christ was supernaturally revealed to him by the Father Himself - "... for flesh and blood hath not revealed it unto thee, but my Father which is in heaven." Only the saved will have a right concept of the Person of Jesus Christ - that He is the Son of God and God, the Son; and that He came to die for our sins, was buried, and rose again bodily the third day.

b. **THE WRONG MESSIAH:** ... Tell us, when shall these things be? and what shall be the sign of thy coming, and of the end of the world? And Jesus answered and said unto them, Take heed that no man deceive you. For many shall come in my name, saying, I am Christ; and shall deceive many... For there shall arise false Christs, and false prophets, and shall shew (show) great signs and wonders; insomuch that, if it were possible, they shall deceive the very elect. - Mt 24:3-5, 24

   i. The Lord Jesus warns us that in the last days, there will be many "false Christs" and they will deceive the

The experience of Christians is not necessarily Christian experience.
- Donald Grey Barnhouse

professing Christians into placing their faith in them. The "Jesus Christ" of the Mormons is one "god" among many "gods". The "Jesus Christ" of the Jehovah Witnesses is Michael the Archangel. The "Jesus Christ" of the Christian Scientists is just a Divine Principle. The "Jesus Christ" of the Roman Catholics is someone who never died for all our sins and that we must keep on doing good works and earning merits to get to heaven - beginning with baptism to the partaking of the Mass, the Confessional, Penance, and finally culminating with the Extreme Unction. Even with that, the poor penitent must necessarily go to purgatory to pay for his "unpaid sins". All these "Jesus Christs" share the same name "Jesus Christ", but they are not the "Jesus Christ" of the Bible. It is like two different persons sharing the same name "John." As a result, these religionists and cultists have no salvation.

3.   A SCRIPTURAL METHOD

   a.   THE RIGHT METHOD - SALVATION BY FAITH:

      i.   **BY GRACE:** For by grace are ye saved through faith; and that not of yourselves: it is the gift of God: Not of works, lest any man should boast. - Eph 2:8-9

         And if by grace, then is it no more of works: otherwise grace is no more grace. But if it be of works, then is it no more grace: otherwise work is no more work. - Rom 11:6

      ii.   **THROUGH FAITH:** Now to him that worketh is the reward not reckoned of grace, but of debt. But to him that worketh not, but believeth on him that justifieth the ungodly, his faith is counted for righteousness. Even as David also describeth the blessedness of the man, unto whom God imputeth righteousness without works. - Rom 4:4-6

         For therein is the righteousness of God revealed from faith to faith: as it is written, The just shall live by faith. - Rom 1:17

We often talk about the courage of our conviction, but do we have the courage to change our conviction when we are wrong?

iii. **IN CHRIST:** ... Sirs, what must I do to be saved? And they said, Believe on the Lord Jesus Christ, and thou shalt be saved, and thy house. - Acts 16:30-31

But as many as received him, to them gave he power to become the sons of God, even to them that believe on his name. - Jn 1:12

b. **THE WRONG METHOD - SALVATION BY WORKS:**

i. **DEPENDING ON GOOD WORKS:** What shall we say then? That the Gentiles, which followed not after righteousness, have attained to righteousness, even the righteousness which is of faith. But Israel, which followed after the law of righteousness, hath not attained to the law of righteousness. Wherefore? Because they sought it not by faith, but as it were by the works of the law. For they stumbled at that stumblingstone. - Rom 9:30-32

ii. **DEPENDING ON SELF-RIGHTEOUSNESS:** Brethren, my heart's desire and prayer to God for Israel is, that they might be saved. For I bear them record that they have a zeal of God, but not according to knowledge. For they being ignorant of God's righteousness, and going about to establish their own righteousness, have not submitted themselves unto the righteousness of God. - Rom 10:1-3

If you be found in your own righteousness you will be lost in your own righteousness. - William Secker

iii. **DEPENDING ON THE KEEPING OF THE LAWS:** Christ is become of no effect unto you, whosoever of you are justified by the law; ye are fallen from grace. - Gal 5:4 / For whosoever shall keep the whole law, and yet offend in one point, he is guilty of all. - Jas 2:10

iv. I believe that the root of almost every schism and heresy from which the Christian church has ever suffered has been the effort of men to earn, rather than to receive, their salvation. - John Ruskin

The devil's best work is done by many who claim to love the Lord.

4. **A SCRIPTURAL MOTIVE**

    a. **THE RIGHT MOTIVE - WE COME TO GOD ON HIS TERMS AND CONDITIONS:**

        i. **THE APOSTLE PAUL:** ... Lord, what wilt thou have me to do?... - Acts 9:6

        ii. **THE PHILIPPIAN JAILOR:** ... Sirs, what must I do to be saved? - Acts 16:30

        iii. **THE THREE THOUSANDS ON THE DAY OF PENTECOST:** ... Men and brethren, what shall we do? - Acts 2:37

    b. **THE WRONG MOTIVE - WE COME TO GOD ON OUR TERMS AND CONDITIONS:**

        i. **BECAUSE OF MONEY:** Then one of the twelve, called Judas Iscariot, went unto the chief priests, And said unto them, What will ye give me, and I will deliver him unto you? And they covenanted with him for thirty pieces of silver. And from that time he sought opportunity to betray him. - Mt 26:14-16

        Judas Iscariot, who was one of the twelve apostles of the Lord Jesus Christ, witnessed practically every miracle Jesus performed, heard most of His sermons and yet died a lost man - "... which Judas by transgression fell, that he might go to his own place." (Acts 1:25) The motive for Judas' belief was money. He believed that the Lord Jesus would come into power as the Jewish Messiah and he, in turn, would be a rich man. However, when the Lord Jesus had proclaimed His imminent death, Judas decided that he might as well betray him for the price of a slave.

        ii. **BECAUSE OF POWER:** And when Simon saw that through laying on of the apostles' hands the Holy Ghost was given, he offered them money. Saying, Give me also this power, that on whomsoever I lay hand, he may receive the Holy Ghost. But Peter said unto him, Thy money perish with thee, because thou hast thought

There is always a good reason and a real reason to everything we do or not do.

that the gift of God may be purchased with money... For I perceive that thou art in the gall of bitterness, and in the bond of iniquity. - Acts 8:18-23

Simon the sorcerer's motive for believing in God was power. He thought that he could purchase that power with money. Likewise, there are many professing Christians who believe in Christ with ulterior motives - because of some Christian lady or man whom they hope to marry one day or some fringe benefits they secretly desire from the church.

5. A SCRIPTURAL MANIFESTATION

a. THE RIGHT MANIFESTATION:

i. **THE DOING OF THE WORKS OF GOD:** Not every one that saith unto me, Lord, Lord, shall enter into the kingdom of heaven; but he that doeth the will of my Father which is in heaven. - Mt 7:21

ii. **THE KEEPING OF THE COMMANDMENTS OF GOD:** And hereby we do know that we know him, if we keep his commandments. - 1 Jn 2:3

iii. **THE MANIFESTATION OF THE RIGHTEOUSNESS OF GOD:** Whosoever is born of God doth not commit sin (does not keep committing sin); for his seed remaineth in him: and he cannot sin (keep on sinning), because he is born of God. - 1 Jn 3:9

iv. Faith justifies the person and works justify his faith. - Elisha Coles

v. We are not justified by doing good works, but being justified we then do good. - William Jenkyn

vi. What saves is faith alone, but the faith that saves is never alone. - J. I. Packer

vii. The law sends us to the gospel, that we may be justified, and the gospel sends us to the law again to enquire what is our duty, being justified. - Samuel Bolton

b. **THE WRONG MANIFESTATION:**

    i. **NOT BEING RIGHTEOUS:** In this the children of God are manifest, and the children of the devil: whosoever doeth not righteousness is not of God, neither he that loveth not his brother. - 1 Jn 3:10

    ii. **NOT DOING GOOD WORKS:** What doth it profit, my brethren, though a man say he hath faith, and have not works? can faith save him? If a brother or sister be naked, and destitute of daily food, And one of you say unto them, Depart in peace, be ye warmed and filled; notwithstanding ye give them not those things which are needful to the body; what doth it profit? Even so faith, if it hath not works, is dead, being alone... For as the body without the spirit is dead, so faith without works is dead also. - Jas 2:14-26

    iii. **NOT KEEPING THE COMMANDMENTS OF GOD:** He that saith, I know him, and keepeth not his commandments, is a liar, and the truth is not in him. - 1 Jn 2:4

    iv. Not depending on good works for salvation is not the same as not displaying good works after salvation. In fact, a truly born-again Christian is very conscientious and careful in fearing and following God.

    v. If any man has a faith which does not produce good works, it is the faith of devils - "Thou believest that there is one God; thou doest well: the devils also believe, and tremble." (Jas 2:19)

    vi. A lady once said to a preacher, "I believe in God. But I don't believe that I need to attend church, read my Bible, pray or give." "Madam," said the preacher, "you don't believe in God, you believe in yourself."

    vii. The person who claims he can live carelessly because he is not under the Law but under grace needs to be sure that he is not under wrath.

The evidence of saving faith is not how much you believe but how well you behave.

CREATION AND THE CREATOR

The Earth is "Anthropic"

"Many scientists today are coming to the conclusion that the earth is "anthropic". By this, they mean that this earth bears evidence that it was designed by an intelligent Being to allow life to exist within a very narrow scientific parameter. The following extract gives us an idea of why this is so:

In researching the size of the earth we discover that the mass and size of the earth are just right. If the earth's diameter were 7,200 miles instead of 8,000, almost the whole earth, due to a lessening of its atmospheric mantle, would be reduced to a snow and ice waste. If there were a variation of only 10 percent, either in the increase or decrease of the size of our world, no life as we know it on earth would be possible! If the average temperature of the earth were raised by two or three degrees you could bid goodbye to many of the big cities of the earth, for the glaciers would melt, and that in turn would flood many of the big cities... The earth's axis, which now points toward the North Star, is tilted just right - at the strange angle of 23 degrees from the perpendicular, that is, in relation to the plane of its orbit. Because of this tilt the sun appears to go north in the summer and south in the winter, giving us four seasons in the temperate zone. For the same reason, there is twice as much of the land area of the earth that can be cultivated and inhabited as there would be if the sun were always over the equator, with no change of seasons. Think what would happen if the earth were tilted any other way than it is. We live miraculously on this planet, protected from eight killer rays from the sun, by a thin layer of ozone high up in our atmosphere. If that little belt of ozone, approximately forty miles up and only one eighth of an inch thick (if compressed), should suddenly drift into space, all life on earth would perish. The first miracle, in the light of what the rest of the universe is like, is that there is an ocean here! In the universe as a whole, liquid water of any kind - sweet or salty - is an exotic rarity. Contrary to common belief,

All that I have seen teaches me to trust the Creator for all I have not seen.

the liquid state is exceptional in nature; most matter in the universe seems to consist either of flaming gases, as in stars, or frozen solids drifting in the abyss of space. The amazing accuracy and smoothness with which the Universe revolves - as a flawless, perfect machine - can be seen in the perfection that characterizes the journey of our earth around the sun. It takes the earth 365 days, 5 hours, 48 minutes and 48 seconds to make its journey around the sun. And in this circuit... the earth has varied in only the slightest degree. None but an infinite GOD could achieve such flawless, continuous perfection. I believe as God states in the Bible (For the invisible things of him from the creation of the world are clearly seen, being understood by the things that are made, even his eternal power and Godhead; so that they are without excuse. - Rom 1:20) that nature and creation itself reveals that there is a Creator. We know that for every design there is a designer, and for every law there is a lawgiver. "In the beginning God created" is still the most up-to-date statement on the origin of the universe and all that it contains." (Duane T. Gish, Ph.D. , Biochemistry, University of California, Berkeley, Adapted from the tract "Have you been brainwashed?", Gospel Tract Distributors)

The Existence of God fits the Facts

"Belief in a self-existent, personal God is in harmony with all the facts of our mental and moral nature, as well as with all the phenomena of the natural world. If God exists, a universal belief in his existence is natural enough; the irresistible impulse to ask for a first cause is accounted for; our religious nature has an object; the uniformity of natural law finds an adequate explanation, and human history is vindicated from the charge of being a vast imposture. Atheism leaves all these matters without an explanation, and makes, not history alone, but our moral and intellectual nature itself, an imposture and a lie." (F. L. Patton)

Footprints in the Sand

"Many years ago an atheistic French scientist was crossing the Sahara desert with an Arab guide. The Arab believed in God and prayer. When he was uncertain of the way, he would kneel and ask God for guidance. This annoyed the scientist. Contemptuously he asked, "How do you know there is a God?" Solemnly the Arab asked, "How do I know that a man

He was in the world, and the world was made by him, and the world knew him not. - Jn 1:10

and not a camel passed by our tent last night in the darkness?" "Why, by his footprints in the sand," said the atheist. "I see God's footprints in the things He has created - the sun, moon and stars. They proclaim His power and greatness! These things just didn't happen!" said the Arab." (W. B. Knight)

Nobody made It

Sir Isaac Newton had a replica of our solar system made in miniature. In the center was the sun with its retinue of planets revolving around it. A scientist entered Newton's study one day, and exclaimed, "My! What an exquisite thing this is! Who made it?" "Nobody!" replied Newton to the questioner who was an unbeliever. "You must think I am a fool. Of course somebody made it, and he is a genius."

Laying his book aside, Newton arose and laid a hand on his friend's shoulder and said: "This thing is but a puny imitation of a much grander system whose laws you and I know, and I am not able to convince you that this mere toy is without a designer and maker; yet you profess to believe that the great original from which the design is taken has come into being without either a designer or maker. Now tell me, by what sort of reasoning do you reach such incongruous conclusions?"

It ought not to be taught in School

One morning I woke up and something had happened in the night, and it struck me that I had been working on this stuff (evolution) for twenty years and there was not one thing I knew about it. That's quite a shock to learn that one can be so misled so long... so for the last few weeks I've tried putting a simple question to various people and groups of people. Question is: Can you tell me anything you know about evolution, any one thing, any one thing that is true? I tried that question on the geology staff at the Field Museum of Natural History and the only answer I got was silence. I tried it on the members of the Evolutionary Morphology Seminar in the University of Chicago, a very prestigious body of evolutionists, and all I got there was silence for a long time and eventually one person said, "I do know one thing - it ought not to be taught in high school." (Dr Colin Patterson, Senior Paleontologist, British Museum of Natural History, London, 5 November, 1981)

For every house is builded by some man; but he that built all things is God. - Heb 3:4

121

SIN AND THE SINNER

Sin has no Logic

"A scorpion, being a poor swimmer, asked a turtle to carry him on his back across a river. "Are you mad?" exclaimed the turtle. "You'll sting me while I'm swimming and I'll drown." "My dear turtle," laughed the scorpion, "if I were to sting you, you would drown and I would go down with you. Now, where is the logic in that?" "You're right," cried the turtle. "Hop on!" The scorpion climbed aboard and halfway across the river gave the turtle a mighty sting. As they both sank to the bottom, the turtle resignedly said, "Do you mind if I ask you something? You said there'd be no logic in your stinging me. Why did you do it?" "It has nothing to do with logic," the drowning scorpion sadly replied. "It is just my character."" (Horizons)

Spiritually Blind

"A minister faithfully proclaimed the gospel in an open-air meeting in Glasgow. At the conclusion of his message, an unbeliever stepped from the crowd and said: "I don't believe what the minister said. I don't believe in heaven or hell. I don't believe in God or Christ. I haven't seen them." Then a man, wearing dark glasses, came forward and said: "You say there is a river near this place - the River Clyde. There is no such thing. You say there are people standing here, but it cannot be true. I haven't seen them - I was born blind! Only a blind man could say what I have said. You are spiritually blind and cannot see. The Bible says of you, "But the natural man receiveth not the things of the Spirit of God: for they are foolishness unto him: neither can he know them, because they are spiritually discerned." (1 Cor 2:14)" (W. B. Knight)

Can't feel the Weight of Sin

A flippant youth asked a preacher, "You say that unsaved people carry a weight of sin. I feel nothing. How heavy is sin? Is it ten pounds? Eighty pounds?" The preacher replied by asking the youth, "If you laid a four-hundred-pound weight on a corpse, would it feel the load?" The youth replied, "It would feel nothing, because it is dead." The preacher concluded,

A secret sin on earth is an open scandal in heaven.

"That spirit, too, is indeed dead which feels no load of sin or is indifferent to its burden and flippant about its presence." The youth was silenced.

The Emperor's New Clothes

Many of us are accustomed to the legendary story "The Emperor's New Clothes". As the story goes, an Emperor desired to impress his people on a certain occasion with some very ethereal garments. He secured the services of two very able tailors in the kingdom who happened to be tricksters out to deceive the Emperor. They presented to the Emperor a make-belief, invisible "garment", and having convinced both the Emperor and his attendants that only the noble and men of good character were able to see this "clothes of grand design", the Emperor put it on and paraded himself before his subjects. Not wanting to appear foolish, everyone pretended to be able to see and admire this "elegant garment". Finally, a little child exclaimed, "The Emperor has no clothes!" In no time, the giggling and laughter of the common folks sent the Emperor back in a hurry to his palace red-faced and very embarrassed by his foolishness. The world too, would pat themselves on the back and assure themselves that they are alright; but, in the eyes of God, we are all like this foolish Emperor, naked in our righteousness before Him - "But we are all as an unclean thing, and all our righteousnesses are as filthy rags..." (Isa 64:6)

Death Tracks

Two men were lost in a blizzard in a forest. They kept walking and after a long while, they chanced upon two pairs of human footprints. They congratulated themselves that they were on the right track to safety. Traveling on, they saw more footprints and were even more sure of finding their way back home. However, a lone Indian who witnessed all this stopped them and warned, "White men, don't follow those tracks. They are your own tracks. You have been going round and round the forest. We call those footprints 'Death Tracks'." In a similar manner, the lost are following their own tracks, going round and round in life, not knowing that these will lead them to a Christless eternity. Their philosophies are: "let us eat, drink and be merry, for tomorrow we die", "do what feels good", "grab all you can in life", "don't think about the future and God, there is no such thing as hell judgment", etc. Soon, like these men who could have followed their own tracks to their death, they will discover that: they are "over the hill", "what you see is not what it appears to be", "after every party is the same emptiness again", "vanity of vanities; all is vanity" (Eccl 1:2), and finally, as they draw their last breath, God will say to them, "Depart from me, ye cursed, into everlasting fire, prepared for the devil and his angels." (Mt 25:41) While we still have the time, let us turn back to the Savior who assures us that, "... the Son of man is come to seek and to save that which was lost." (Lk 19:10)

The Valley of the Blind

A story was told of a mysterious disease which caused the people living in a said valley to go blind. Adding to their plight was an earthquake which cut off civilization from their village. Over time, each successive generation was born blind. The story continued with a man from the outside world who accidentally fell into this valley. The first thing he noticed was that the people were sightless and their homes were without windows. The villagers moved around in lines by holding on to each other's shoulders. The first thought that came to his mind was, "In the Country of the Blind the One-Eyed Man is King." Instead of taking advantage of these blind people, he found himself surrounded by them. Apparently, they could hear very well with their ears his every movement. Having been eventually apprehended by these blind folks, the man told them about sight, colors, the clouds, et al. But they thought he was crazy as they had never heard of such things. Eventually, he stayed with them and fell in love with a beautiful maiden. When he asked for her hand, they (the blind community) would only agree if he would remove his eyes in order to get rid of his "crazy ideas" of sight and colors. The story ended with the man finally escaping from this valley of the blind. We act like these folks because of our spiritual blindness - instead of loving God and hating sins, we end up loving sins and hating God. Instead of walking in the light of God's truth, we prefer to be in spiritual darkness - "And this is the condemnation, that light is come into the world, and men loved darkness rather than light, because their deeds were evil." (Jn 3:19)

We all come from the same mould - and some of us are mouldier than others!

DEATH AND THE JUDGMENT OF GOD

A Strange Encounter with Death

An old legend tells of a merchant in Baghdad who, one day sent his servant to the market. Before very long the servant came back, white and trembling, and in great agitation said to his master, "Down in the market place I was jostled by a woman in the crowd, and when I turned around I saw it was Death that jostled me. She looked at me and made a threatening gesture. Master, please lend me your horse, for I must hasten away to avoid her. I will ride to Samarra and there I will hide, and Death will not find me." The merchant lent him his horse and the servant galloped away in great haste. Later the merchant went down to the market place and saw Death standing in the crowd. He went over to her and asked, "Why did you make a threatening gesture at my servant?" "That was not a threatening gesture," Death said. "It was only a start of surprise. I was astonished to see him in Baghdad, for I have an appointment with him tonight in Samarra."

A Covenant with Death

A man once made a covenant with Death. The covenant was that Death should not come on him unawares - that Death was to give warning of his approach. Years rolled on, and at last Death stood before his victim. The old man blanched and faltered out, "Why, Death you have not been true to your promise, you have not kept your covenant. You promised not to come unannounced. You never gave me any warning." "Not so!" came the answer. "Every one of those gray hairs was a warning; every one of your lost teeth was a warning; your eyes growing dim was a warning; your natural power and vigor abated - that was, a warning. Aha! I've warned you - I've warned you continually." And Death would not delay, but swept his victim into eternity.

Mercy not Justice

An aged Negro was arraigned. In court, charges of a serious nature were placed against him. As court preliminaries were getting under way, it was evident to the young lawyer that his client was ill at ease and under

The peace of the world stems more from the ignorance of the coming judgment than from any real assurance of salvation.

125

great tension. In his effort to impart comfort to the man and allay his fears, the young lawyer said, "Charlie, you need not have any fear. I'm going to see that you get justice in this court today!" A meditative look displaced the hitherto look of fright on the man's face. In measured words, he said, "White man, it isn't justice that I want in this court today. It's mercy!" - Rev. T. F. Callaway

The Bigger Fool

A king sent for his jester one day, and presented him with a stick. He said, "Take this stick and keep it until you find a bigger fool than yourself." Lying on his deathbed, the king again sent for his jester. "I am going away," the king said. "Whither?" asked the jester. "To another country," replied the king. "What provision has your majesty made for this journey and for living in the country whither thou goest?" the jester asked. "None," was the answer. The jester handed the king the stick. "Take it," he said. "I have found a bigger fool than myself, for I only trifle with the things of time while you trifled with things of eternity." - Gospel Herald

Sincerely Wrong

A nurse on night duty in a great hospital in Chicago mistakenly gave a lethal dose of wrong medicine to a little boy. Her error was not detected until it was too late to save his life. Was she not sincere in what she did? Certainly! Was she not conscientiously performing her duties? Certainly! She was sincerely - wrong! She was conscientiously - wrong! Many sincerely say, "All religions are good. They all lead to heaven." Many say, "Let your conscience be your guide. If your conscience tells you a thing is all right, it is O.K." But they all are wrong! All religions are not good. All religions do not lead to heaven. There is only one way to heaven. Jesus said, "I am the way, the truth, and the life: no man cometh unto the Father, but by me." (Jn 14:6) - W. B. Knight

No Escape by Silencing the Messenger

An African chief had done something for which the English government wished to punish him and sent a gunboat for this purpose. A runner

Most men do not fear death; they only pray that they will not be there when it happens.

brought him word that the boat had entered the river. He had the courier killed. The next day a second runner arrived to tell him how far the boat had come up the river. This poor fellow also lost his head. And the same fate was met by the other couriers who arrived the following days. This did not, however, keep the English boat away nor delay the day of judgment. Suddenly the jungle echoed with thunder of cannon and the huts of his kraal collapsed as if made of cardboard. How do we treat the messengers of God who come to tell us of approaching judgment? We may have silenced them, but the judgment day is coming. You may have silenced your conscience, grieved the Holy Spirit, left unopened the Holy Bible, and turned your back to your Christian friends - but the judgment day is coming. - The Sunday School Times

The Violin Player

A probably fictitious story was told of a man who could not play violin. He joined an orchestra and pretended to play with them. He would fake all the movements to look like he knew how. This went along for a while till one day he was required to give a personal audition. For this, he ran off. Today, we merge with the crowds. We do the things they do. We talk their talk. But some day, we will have to stand before God alone. Are we ready to give an account of ourselves before God? We live in crowds but we die one by one. "And I saw the dead, small and great, stand before God; and the books were opened... and the dead were judged out of those things which were written in the books, according to their works... And whosoever was not found written in the book of life was cast into the lake of fire." (Rev 20:12-15)

How shall we Escape?

A Welsh minister, beginning his sermon, leaned over the pulpit and said with a solemn air, "Friends, I have a question to ask. I cannot answer it. You cannot answer it. If an angel from heaven were here, he could not answer it. If a devil from hell were here, he could not answer it." Every eye was fixed on the speaker, who proceeded, "The question is this, how shall we escape, if we neglect so great salvation?" (Heb 2:3)

George Wilson must be Hanged

About the year 1830, a man named George Wilson killed a government employee who caught him in the act of robbing the mails. He was tried and sentenced to be hanged. However, President Andrew Jackson sent him a pardon. But Wilson did a strange thing. He refused to accept the pardon, and no one knew what to do. So the case was carried to the Supreme Court. Chief Justice Marshall, perhaps one of the greatest justices ever, wrote the court's opinion. In it he said, "A pardon is a slip of paper, the value of which is determined by the acceptance of the person to be pardoned. If it is refused, it is no pardon. George Wilson must be hanged." And so he was.

He always said He would Retire

He always said he would retire,
When he had made a million clear,
And so he toiled into the dusk,
From day to day, from year to year!
At last he put his ledgers up,
And laid his stock reports aside,
And when he started out to live,
He found he had already died! - Selected

Found on a Tombstone

Pause, Stranger, when you pass me by,
As you are now, so once was I.
As I am now, so you will be,
So prepare for death and follow me.

All offences against God will either be forgiven or avenged. - A. W. Tozer

GOD'S LOVE AND PROVISION

Eluding God's Rescue

In 1981, a Minnesota radio station reported a story about a stolen car in California. Police were staging an intense search for the vehicle and the driver, even to the point of placing announcements on local radio stations to contact the thief. On the front seat of the stolen car sat a box of crackers that, unknown to the thief, were laced with poison. The car owner had intended to use the crackers as a rat bait. Now the police and the owner of the VW Bug were more interested in apprehending the thief to save his life than to recover the car. So often, when we run from God, we feel it is to escape his punishment. But what we are actually doing is eluding his rescue. - Craig Brian Larson

Rescue of the "Squalas"

The submarine Squalas and its crew lay helpless at the bottom of the Atlantic Ocean, two hundred and forty feet below the surface. The crew sent up smoke flares, hoping that their location would become known. The submarine Sculpin did locate them. A ten-ton diving bell was lowered several times, bringing to safety the thirty-three surviving members of the crew of the ill-fated Squalas. Not one of the thirty-three men said to their rescuers, "I will think it over," or "I will wait for a more convenient season," or "There is too much to give up." All instantly and gratefully accepted the means of escape from death. - Robert G. Lee

The War is Over

In the Philippines, a newspaper once ran a story about a Japanese soldier, Lt. Hiroo Onoda, who had hidden in the jungles to escape capture after Japan lost the war in 1945. For 29 years, he had been living in fear and eluding capture not knowing that the war had ended. He was finally discovered on March 19, 1972, and was told that the war had ended some thirty years ago. He must have felt he had wasted those precious years unnecessarily. He was flown back to Japan, grateful to be reunited with his family again. Likewise, when Jesus died on the cross for our sins, the "war" between God and man was over - man now can be reconciled to God through the sacrifice of our Lord Jesus Christ. But like this Japanese soldier, many sinners are still running and hiding away from God unnecessarily, not knowing that they can be saved through the Lord Jesus Christ.

The Dream

A man once dreamt that he was transported back in time to witness the crucifixion of Jesus Christ. In his dream, he saw how the crowds jeered at the Savior and the Roman soldiers lashed Him. The agonies and cries of the Lord Jesus Christ so moved him that, in his dream, he lunged forward to prevent the soldier from hurting Him. As he jerked at the soldier's back, he got the shock of his life - for he saw that he was that soldier who was whipping Christ! At the end of the day, it was not the Romans that crucified the Lord Jesus Christ or the Jews that demanded His death, but it was you and I who caused Him to be nailed on the cruel cross at Calvary. "But he was wounded for our transgressions, he was bruised for our iniquities: the chastisement of our peace was upon him; and with his stripes we are healed." (Isa 53:5)

Don't you care that my Son died for You?

Back in the days of the Great Depression, a Missouri man named John Griffith was the controller of a great railroad drawbridge across the Mississippi River. One day in the summer of 1937 he decided to take his eight-year-old son, Greg, with him to work. At noon, John Griffith put the bridge up to allow ships to pass and sat on the observation deck with his son to eat lunch. Time passed quickly. Suddenly he was startled by the shrieking of a train whistle in the distance. He quickly looked at his watch and noticed it was 1:07 - the Memphis Express, with four hundred passengers on board, was roaring toward the raised bridge! He leaped from the observation deck and ran back to the control tower. Just before throwing the master lever he glanced down for any ships below. There a sight caught his eye that caused his heart to leap poundingly into his throat. Greg had slipped from the observation deck and had fallen into the massive gears that operate the bridge. His left leg was caught in the cogs of the two main gears! Desperately John's

He that is good at making excuses is seldom good at anything else.
- Benjamin Franklin

mind whirled to devise a rescue plan. But as soon as he thought of a possibility he knew there was no way it could be done. Again, with alarming closeness, the train whistle shrieked in the air. He could hear the clicking of the locomotive wheels over the tracks. That was his son down there - yet there were four hundred passengers on the train. John knew what he had to do, so he buried his head in his left arm and pushed the master switch forward. That great massive bridge lowered into place just as the Memphis Express began to roar across the river. When John Griffith lifted his head with his face smeared with tears, he looked into the passing windows of the train. There were businessmen casually reading their afternoon papers, finely dressed ladies in the dining car sipping coffee, and children pushing long spoons into their dishes of ice cream. No one looked at the control house, and no one looked at the great gearbox. With wrenching agony, John Griffith cried out at the steel train: "I sacrifice my son for you people! Don't you care?" The train rushed by, but nobody heard the father's words, which recalled Lamentation 1:12: "Is it nothing to you, all who pass by?" - Dr James Kennedy, quoted from Illustrations for Biblical Preaching, Michael P. Green, Baker Book House.

Where is the Road?

A traveler engaged a guide to take him across a desert area. When the two men arrived at the edge of the desert, the traveler, looking ahead, saw before him trackless sands without a single footprint, path, or marker of any kind. Turning to his guide, he asked in a tone of surprise, "Where is the road?" With a reproving glance, the guide replied, "I am the road." So, too, is the Lord our way through unfamiliar territory.

The things Undone

It is not the things you do, friend,
It's the things you left undone,
That cause the heartache,
At the setting sun.

If Jesus died for us, how can we live like we owe Him nothing?

SALVATION BY FAITH IN JESUS CHRIST

Use the Key

An old parable said, "A silly servant who was told to open the door set his shoulder to it and pushed with all his might; but the door stirred not, and he could not enter, use what strength he might. Another came with a key and easily unlocked the door and entered right readily." Those who would be saved by works are pushing at heaven's gate without result; but faith is the key that opens the gate at once. - Adapted

Wesley's Ignorance

A humble Moravian workman asked John Wesley before his conversion the searching question, "Do you hope to be saved?" "Yes, I do," replied Wesley. "On what ground do you hope for salvation?" asked the Moravian. "Because of my endeavors to serve God," said Wesley. The Moravian made no reply. He only shook his head and walked silently away. Wesley, in speaking of the incident later said, "I thought him very uncharitable, saying in my heart, 'Would he rob me of my endeavors?'" Later, Wesley saw the light - that salvation is solely of grace, "not by works of righteousness which we have done" (Tit 3:5), or can do. He saw what his brother, Charles, saw and expressed in these words:

Could my tears forever flow,
Could my zeal no languor know,
These for sin could not atone;
Thou must save, and Thou alone:
In my hand no price I bring,
Simply to Thy cross I cling.
- W. B. Knight

Morality may keep you out of jail, but it takes the blood of Jesus Christ to keep you out of hell. - C. H. Spurgeon

Only two Religions

While presenting the Gospel on the streets of a Californian city, we were often interrupted about as follows: "Look here, sir! There are hundreds of religions in this country, and the followers of each sect think theirs is the only right one. How can poor, plain men like us find out what really is the truth?" We generally replied something like this: "Hundreds of religions, you say? That's strange; I've heard of only two." "Oh, but you surely know there are more than that?" "Not at all, Sir, I find, I admit, many shades of difference in the opinions of those comprising the two great schools; but after all there are but two. The one covers all who expect salvation by doing; the other, all who have been saved by something done. So you see the whole question is very simple. Can you save yourself, or must you be saved by another? If you can be your own savior, you do not need my message. If you cannot, you may well listen to it." - H. A. Ironside

The Captor and the Captive

An ancient fable once told of a sovereign who held a prisoner at his will in his castle. One night, wishing to be malevolent, he said to the prisoner, "I will give you a chance to escape. You have one night to do so. There is a way out of this place." Having said that, he left him. The hopeful prisoner felt his way around his cell and discovered a hidden panel which eventually led him from one secret passage to another. He spent the whole night searching eagerly for a way out of his prison. Upon daybreak, he stumbled into his own cell again. The door flung open and the sovereign announced, "I have given you a chance to escape but you failed." "You lied," cried the prisoner, "there is no way out!" "There is," came the reply, "I did not lock the door of your cell last night and you could have just walked out a free man." Just like this nameless prisoner, we too, tend to think that the salvation of God is something complex, like the doing of endless good works, or through some extreme personal sacrifice, or prolonged and intense meditation, or some esoteric and mystical practices, et al. But the way of salvation ordained by God is incredibly simple, like the possibility of this prisoner going through an unlocked door - "... Sirs, what must I do to be saved? And they said, Believe on the Lord Jesus Christ, and thou shalt be saved... " (Acts 16:30-31

Half-Century learning 3 Things

D. L. Moody told: "An old man got up in one of our meetings and said, "I have been forty-two years learning three things." I pricked up my ears at that. I thought if I could find out in three minutes what a man had taken forty-two years to learn, I should like to do it. The first thing he said he had learned was that he could do nothing toward his own salvation. "Well," I said to myself, "that is worth learning." The second thing he found out was that God did not require him to do anything. Well, that was worth finding out, too. And the third thing was that the Lord Jesus Christ had done it all, that salvation was finished, and that all he had to do was to take it. Dear friends, let us learn this lesson. Let us give up our struggling and striving, and accept salvation at once." - Moody Monthly

Lord, Send the Rattlesnakes

There was a farmer who had three sons: Jim, John, and Sam. No one in the family ever attended church or had time for God. The pastor and the others in the church tried for years to interest the family in the things of God but to no avail. Then one day Sam was bitten by a rattlesnake. The doctor was called and he did all he could to help Sam, but the outlook for Sam's recovery was very dim indeed. So the pastor was called to appraise the situation. The pastor arrived, and began to pray as follows: "O wise and righteous Father, we thank Thee that in Thine wisdom thou didst send this rattlesnake to bite Sam. He has never been inside the church and it is doubtful that he has, in all this time, ever prayed or even acknowledged Thine existence. Now we trust that this experience will be a valuable lesson to him and will lead to his genuine repentance. And now, O Father, wilt thou send another rattlesnake to bite Jim, and another to bite John, and another really big one to bite the old man. For years we have done everything we know to get them to turn to Thee, but all in vain. It seems, therefore, that what all our combined efforts could not do, this rattlesnake has done. We thus conclude that the only thing that will do this family any real good is rattlesnake; so, Lord, send us bigger and better rattlesnakes. Amen."

Until you are free to die, you are not free to live.

SOUL-WINNERS AND SOUL-WINNING

Why don't you Hurry?

When a father, who lived on the Western prairies, came home one night, his little boy ran through the long grass to meet him. Suddenly the boy disappeared. Running through the grass to the point where his boy vanished, the man heard a gurgling cry. His son had fallen into an old well. The father barely reached the well in time to save his boy. When the lad revived from his fright, he asked, "O Daddy, why didn't you hurry?" Said the father later, "That boy's question made a missionary out of me. I seemed to hear the piteous, pleading cry of myriad in the regions beyond, "Why don't you hurry? We are dying without God and without hope. Why don't you hurry with the gospel?"

Could it be your Son?

Some years ago, Dr. Daniel Poling returned home after an absence of a few days. He entered a taxicab. As he rode along, the taxi driver, who did not know Dr. Poling, asked, "Have you heard about the boys who are adrift in a rowboat, and who, at latest reports, have not been found?" "No," replied Dr. Poling, seemingly not too much concerned. Then he added, "The boys should have been more careful." After a moment, he asked, "Do you know the names of the boys?" "No, not all of them. I know only one. His name is Poling." Instantly Dr Poling became all attention as it dawned upon him that one of the lost youths was his own boy! Oh, that we could feel deeply moved toward every lost soul, taking each upon our hearts, and doing everything to bring him to Christ. - Rev. C. Leslie Miller

The Joy of Salvation

Bruce Crozier, a seven-year-old boy, wandered from his father's hunting camp in Arizona. He was lost for six days and six nights. At last he was found, thirty-two miles from the camp. When the mother embraced him, she exclaimed, "It is almost impossible to believe I have my boy back!" Then she fainted. The father, who had directed a thousand searchers for the boy from his hunting camp, received by phone the joyous news, and he, too, lapsed into unconsciousness. We cannot measure the greatness of the joy of that mother and father. Nor can we measure the

"joy in the presence of the angels of God over one sinner that repented."
- Adapted from Now

In the Morning, Sow thy Seed!

Years ago, in the city of Toronto, Canada, a young man passed a street meeting. He heard only one verse from the Bible: "Son, give me thine heart." At the time, the verse apparently went in one ear and out the other. More than fifty years later, the verse, which had lain dormant in his heart, became accusingly and convictively alive. Then he fell on his knees, crying to God for His mercy and forgiveness. Let us be alert and aggressive in obeying the command, "In the morning sow thy seed, and in the evening withhold not thine hand: for thou knowest not whether shall prosper, either this or that, or whether they both shall be alike good." (Eccl 11:6) Even the weakest and unworthiest ones may sow the seed, remembering that the life lies not in the sower, but in the seed! - W. B. Knight

Man on the Railway Track

Dr. John McNeill once told a group of ministers how he had come upon a drunken man fast asleep between the railway tracks - and the midnight express was due. "What would you have done?" he demanded of the ministers. One said, "Man, I would get him off the track. I would not be mild in dealing with him. I would not invite him to get himself off. I would be rough and seize him, and by my strength I would drag him off though I dropped exhausted by his side." "Even so," said McNeill, "that is the state of every unsaved soul - asleep between the tracks, and God's judgment express is almost due." - United Evangelical

The Blind Man going over the Cliff

Suppose I were to see a blind man unknowingly approaching the brink of a high precipice, and that I were to sit by without concern or any effort to warn or save him from certain death, would I not be as guilty of his death in God's sight as though I had murdered him outright? The death of a body, which might have been (but was not) prevented, is a terrible thing, but what about the preventable death of a human soul - perchance of many souls - for which God may hold me responsible?
- Alan Redpath

Never has a man's eternity depends so much on the voice of another.

Indifferent Christians

Some Africans were getting on a riverboat, carrying in their hands sacks and baskets of vegetables. They were going to market. One of them slipped and fell into the water. She grabbed for the side of the boat and held on until her fingers became numb. Finally she could hold on no longer and sank beneath the turgid waters. Not one native made a move to rescue her. They were stonily indifferent to her cries for help. When the boat captain learned what had happened, he swore and cursed at the heartless natives. "Why didn't you reach down and lift her from the water?" he asked. They replied in chorus, "If we had, what would have become of our fruits and vegetables?" Before we pass judgment on these cruel, benighted heathen, let us do a bit of heart-searching. All around us are those who are going into eternity without God and without hope - forever lost. Too many Christians sing about rescuing the perishing, but do little or nothing about it. - Told by a missionary

Is it True, Madam, that You are not a Missionary?

Dr. Wilfred Grenfell, medical missionary to Labrador, was guest at a dinner in London, together with a number of socially prominent British men and women. During the course of the dinner, the lady seated next to him turned and said, "Is it true Dr. Grenfell, that you are a missionary?" Dr. Grenfell looked at her for a moment before replying, "Is it true, madam, that you are not?"

Whose Responsibility is It?

Some years ago there was a shipwreck off the Pacific Northwest coast. A crowd of fishermen in a nearby village gathered to watch the ship as it was smashed on the rocks. A lifeboat was sent to the rescue, and after a terrific struggle, the rescuers came back with all of the shipwrecked sailors but one.

"There was no room in the lifeboat for him, so we told him to stay by the ship and someone would come back for him," one of the rescuers explained. "Who will come with me?" shouted a young man from the crowd.

Just then a little old lady cried out, "Don't go, Jim, my son. Don't go. You are all I have left. Your father was drowned in the sea; your brother William sailed away and we've never heard from him; and now if you are lost, I'll be left alone. Oh, Jim, please don't go."

Winners of souls must first be weepers of souls.

Jim listened patiently to his mother's pleading, then said, "Mother, I must go! It is my duty. I must go!" The onlookers watched as the men in the lifeboat fought their way back toward the wreck. Anxiously Jim's mother wept and prayed. They saw the boat heading back to shore, a frail little shell tossed about by the waves. At last when the boat came close enough to hear, those on shore shouted, "Did you get him?" And Jim shouted back, "Yes, and tell Mother it's her son William!"

The Starfish

I awoke early, as I often did, just before sunrise to walk by the ocean's edge and greet the new day. As I moved through the misty dawn, I focused on a faint, far away motion. I saw a youth, bending and reaching and flailing arms, dancing on the beach, no doubt in celebration of the perfect day soon to begin.

As I approached, I sadly realized that the youth was not dancing to the bay, but rather bending to sift through the debris left by the night's tide, stopping now and then to pick up a starfish and then standing, to heave it back into the sea. I asked the youth the purpose of the effort. "The tide has washed the starfish onto the beach and they cannot return to the sea by themselves," the youth replied. "When the sun rises, they will die, unless I throw them back to the sea."

As the youth explained, I surveyed the vast expanse of beach, stretching in both directions beyond my sight. Starfish littered the shore in numbers beyond calculation. The hopelessness of the youth's plan became clear to me and I countered, "But there are more starfish on this beach than you can ever save before the sun is up. Surely you cannot expect to make a difference."

The youth paused briefly to consider my words, bent to pick up a starfish and threw it as far as possible. Turning to me he simply said, "I made a difference to that one."

I left the boy and went home, deep in thought of what the boy had said. I returned to the beach and spent the rest of the day helping the boy throw starfish in to the sea. - Based on the story by Loren Eisley

A man's religion may well be suspected when he is content to go to heaven alone. - J. C. Ryle

THE POTENTIAL IN PERSONAL EVANGELISM

1. **IT CAN BE DONE BY ANYONE**

   a. In the average church only a few can preach or teach effectively, but any saved person can be a soul-winner. It is not that we cannot but we would not.

2. **IT CAN BE DONE IN ANY PLACE**

   a. Some places you cannot preach. Soul-winning can be done any place - as long as two people can come together - at home, school or work.

3. **IT CAN BE DONE AT ANY TIME**

   a. The time for church service is limited. Personal evangelism can be done 24 hours a day, 7 days a week.

4. **IT REACHES ALL CLASSES OF PEOPLE**

   a. Some people cannot come to church - the shut-ins, sick or shift workers. Some people won't come to church. Personal evangelism can reach out to all these people.

5. **IT HITS THE MARK**

   a. It is almost impossible for a preacher to reach every heart every time he preaches. Personal evangelism is geared towards meeting the personal needs of the individual.

6. **IT WORKS WHEN ALL ELSE FAILS**

   a. Many attend Sunday School, church, evangelistic meetings and leave without understanding salvation. Many times church services are impersonal. Personal evangelism shows personal concern for the individual.

7. **IT PRODUCES LARGE RESULTS**

   a. Great churches are built on soul-winning by soul-winners. If 100 members were to take upon themselves to win 1 soul in one month, there would be 200 believers in the next month, and 1,200 converts in one year.

Soul-winners are like mosquitoes. They do not wait for an opening. They create the openings for doing soul-winning.

THE PREREQUISITE IN PERSONAL EVANGELISM

1. <u>**HE OUGHT TO BE A SAVED MAN**</u>

   a. Jesus answered and said unto them, Verily, verily, I say unto thee, Except a man be born again, he cannot see the kingdom of God. - Jn 3:3

2. <u>**HE OUGHT TO BE A SCRIPTURAL MAN**</u>

   a. Study to shew (show) thyself approved unto God, a workman that needeth not to be ashamed, rightly dividing the word of truth. - 2 Tim 2:15

3. <u>**HE OUGHT TO BE A SANCTIFIED MAN**</u>

   a. If a man therefore purge himself from these, he shall be a vessel unto honour, sanctified, and meet for the master's use, and prepared unto every good work. - 2 Tim 2:21

4. <u>**HE OUGHT TO BE A SUBSERVIENT MAN**</u>

   a. And he saith unto them, Follow me, and I will make you fishers of men. - Mt 4:19

5. <u>**HE OUGHT TO BE A SPIRIT-FILLED MAN**</u>

   a. And when they had prayed, the place was shaken where they were assembled together; and they were all filled with the Holy Ghost, and they spake the word of God with boldness. - Acts 4:31

6. <u>**HE OUGHT TO BE A SURRENDERED MAN**</u>

   a. I am crucified with Christ: nevertheless I live; yet not I, but Christ liveth in me: and the life which I now live in the flesh I live by the faith of the Son of God, who loved me, and gave himself for me. - Gal 2:20

7. <u>**HE OUGHT TO BE A SINGLE-MINDED MAN**</u>

   a. But none of these things move me, neither count I my life dear unto myself, so that I might finish my course with joy, and the ministry, which I have received of the Lord Jesus, to testify the gospel of the grace of God. - Acts 20:24

Thy hands, the means to make another clean, must not themselves be dirty.

THE PROPRIETY IN PERSONAL EVANGELISM

1.   **THE DO'S IN PERSONAL EVANGELISM.**

   a.   **BE PATIENT:**   And the servant of the Lord must not strive; but be gentle unto all men, apt to teach, patient, In meekness instructing those that oppose themselves; if God peradventure (perhaps) will give them repentance to the acknowledging of the truth. - 2 Tim 2:24-25

   b.   **BE POSITIVE:**   For I am with thee, and no man shall set on thee to hurt thee: for I have much people in this city. - Acts 18:10

   c.   **BE PREPARED:**   Study to shew thyself approved unto God, a workman that needeth not to be ashamed, rightly dividing the word of truth. - 2 Tim 2:15

   d.   **BE PERTINENT:** For though I be free from all men, yet have I made myself servant unto all, that I might gain the more. And unto the Jews I became as a Jew, that I might gain the Jews... To the weak became I as weak, that I might gain the weak: I am made all things to all men, that I might by all means save some. And this I do for the gospel's sake, that I might be partaker thereof with you. - 1 Cor 9:19-23

   e.   **BE PRAYERFUL:** Withal praying also for us, that God would open unto us a door of utterance, to speak the mystery of Christ, for which I am also in bonds. - Col 4:3

   f.   **BE PERCEPTIVE:**   And my speech and my preaching was not with enticing words of man's wisdom, but in demonstration of the Spirit and of power: That your faith should not stand in the wisdom of men, but in the power of God. - 1 Cor 2:4-5

   g.   **BE PERSEVERING:** They that sow in tears shall reap in joy. He that goeth forth and weepeth, bearing precious seed, shall doubtless come again with rejoicing, bringing his sheaves with him. - Psa 126:5-6

The way of God to a human heart is through a human heart.
- Samuel Gordon

141

2. THE DON'TS IN PERSONAL EVANGELISM.

a. Don't be guilty of having body odor or bad breath.

b. Don't be self-righteous by talking down to the sinner.

c. Don't embarrass him by dealing with him in front of others.

d. Don't get sidetracked. Stay on the main subject concerning salvation.

e. Don't put him on the defensive by condemning his religion or opinions.

f. Don't evangelize during working hours without the prospect's consent.

g. Don't interrupt another personal worker who is evangelizing unless you are asked to do so.

h. Don't argue. Agree with him or say, "I will answer that question later." We can disagree without being disagreeable.

i. Don't rush your prospects to make a decision if they are not ready. Never use high pressure tactics or "pluck green fruits" (unripe fruits). They may say "yes" to you just to get rid of you or you may end up with your "converts" instead of the Lord's converts.

j. Don't get familiar with the opposite sex. Do not practice 'evangelism dating'. Let us do all things with a right motive - to win soul and to glorify God.

k. Don't be discouraged by initial failures or incompetence in sharing the gospel. A bad attempt is better than no attempt. We gain experience and get better with each successive attempt.

l. Don't wear out your welcome. Don't stay so long that you make him hate you - "Withdraw thy foot from thy neighbour's house; lest he be weary of thee, and so hate thee." (Prov 25:17) Do give yourself and others another chance to reach out to him.

THE PRIORITY IN PERSONAL EVANGELISM

1. **THE HARVEST IS PLENTEOUS:** Then saith he unto his disciples, The harvest truly is plenteous... - Mt 9:37

   The tragedy of our generation is that untold millions are still untold.

2. **THE LABOURERS ARE FEW:** ... but the labourers are few; Pray ye therefore the Lord of the harvest, that he will send forth labourers into his harvest. - Mt 9:37-38

   It is often said that it is difficult to get sinners in - but it is often just as difficult to get the saints out.

3. **THE COMMANDMENT IS SPECIFIC:** And he said unto them, Go ye into all the world, and preach the gospel to every creature. - Mk 16:15

   We can never take the gospel to the wrong address - "Go ye into all the world..."

4. **THE TIME IS SHORT:** I must work the works of him that sent me, while it is day: the night cometh, when no man can work. - Jn 9:4

   The gospel is the good news only if it arrives in time. - Carl F. H. Henry

5. **THE SOULS ARE PERISHING:** And in hell he lift up his eyes, being in torments... And he cried and said, Father Abraham, have mercy on me, and send Lazarus, that he may dip the tip of his finger in water, and cool my tongue; for I am tormented in this flame. - Lk 16:23-24

   The church is not a yachting club but a fleet of fishing boats.

6. **THE WORK IS NOW:** Say not ye, There are yet four months, and then cometh harvest? behold, I say unto you, Lift up your eyes, and look on the fields; for they are white (ripe) already to harvest. - Jn 4:35

   When we are in the wrong place, our right place is empty.

7. **THE LORD IS PLEADING:** Also I heard the voice of the Lord, saying, Whom shall I send, and who will go for us? Then said I, Here am I; send me. - Isa 6:8

    The only one among the twelve apostles who did not become a missionary, became a traitor. - Gospel Herald

8. **THE GUILT IS GREAT:** When I say unto the wicked, Thou shalt surely die; and thou givest him not warning, nor speakest to warn the wicked from his wicked way, to save his life; the same wicked man shall die in his iniquity; but his blood will I require at thine hand. - Ezek 3:18

    Not to do what we ought to do is as bad as doing what we ought not to do. - George W. Truett

    We are either fulfilling the Great Commission or committing the Great Omission.

9. **THE TASK IS URGENT:** Preach the word; be instant in season, out of season; reprove, rebuke, exhort with all longsuffering and doctrine. - 2 Tim 4:2

    In witnessing, silence is not golden. Sometimes, it's just plain yellow (cowardice).

10. **THE JOY IS TREMENDOUS:** Likewise, I say unto you, there is joy in the presence of the angels of God over one sinner that repenteth. - Lk 15:10

    For what is our hope, or joy, or crown of rejoicing? Are not even ye in the presence of our Lord Jesus Christ at his coming? - 1 Thess 2:19

11. **THE REWARD IS ETERNAL:** ... and they that turn many to righteousness as the stars for ever and ever. - Dan 12:3

    One soul is worth more than the riches of this world put together - "For what shall it profit a man, if he shall gain the whole world, and lose his own soul?" (Mk 8:36)

Every life without Christ is a mission field; every life with Christ is a missionary.

THE POSSIBILITY IN PERSONAL EVANGELISM

1. **BECAUSE OF GOD'S POWER:** And Jesus came and spake unto them, saying, All power is given unto me in heaven and in earth. Go ye therefore, and teach all nations... - Mt 28:18-19

2. **BECAUSE OF GOD'S PRAYER:** Neither pray I for these alone, but for them also which shall believe on me through their word. - Jn 17:20

3. **BECAUSE OF GOD'S PEOPLE:** But ye shall receive power, after that the Holy Ghost is come upon you: and ye shall be witnesses unto me both in Jerusalem, and in all Judaea, and in Samaria, and unto the uttermost part of the earth. - Acts 1:8

4. **BECAUSE OF GOD'S PROMISE:** And other sheep I have, which are not of this fold: them also I must bring, and they shall hear my voice; and there shall be one fold, and one shepherd. - Jn 10:16

5. **BECAUSE OF GOD'S PASSION:** For God so loved the world, that he gave his only begotten Son... - Jn 3:16

6. **BECAUSE OF GOD'S PRESENCE:** Then the Spirit said unto Philip, Go near, and join thyself to this chariot... Then Philip opened his mouth, and began at the same scripture, and preached unto him Jesus. - Acts 8:29, 35

7. **BECAUSE OF GOD'S POTENTIAL:** But Jesus beheld them, and said unto them, With men this is impossible; but with God all things are possible. - Mt 19:26

8. **BECAUSE OF GOD'S PATIENCE:** The Lord is not slack concerning his promise, as some men count slackness; but is longsuffering to us-ward, not willing that any should perish, but that all should come to repentance. - 2 Pet 3:9

9. **BECAUSE OF GOD'S PROTECTION:** ... for he hath said, I will never leave thee, nor forsake thee. So that we may boldly say, The Lord is my helper, and I will not fear what man shall do unto me. - Heb 13:5-6

The secret of reaching men is to know the secret of reaching God.

10. **BECAUSE OF GOD'S "PREACHING":** For after that in the wisdom of God the world by wisdom knew not God, it pleased God by the foolishness of preaching to save them that believe. - 1 Cor 1:21

11. **BECAUSE OF GOD'S PROVISION:** And Moses said unto the LORD, O my Lord, I am not eloquent, neither heretofore, nor since thou hast spoken unto thy servant: but I am slow of speech, and of a slow tongue. And the LORD said unto him, Who hath made man's mouth? or who maketh the dumb, or deaf, or the seeing, or the blind? have not I the LORD? Now therefore go, and I will be with thy mouth, and teach thee what thou shalt say. - Exod 4:10-12

12. **BECAUSE OF GOD'S PROVIDENCE:** So shall my word be that goeth forth out of my mouth: it shall not return unto me void, but it shall accomplish that which I please, and it shall prosper in the thing whereto I sent it. - Isa 55:11

13. **BECAUSE OF GOD'S PROPHECY:** And this gospel of the kingdom shall be preached in all the world for a witness unto all nations; and then shall the end come. - Mt 24:14

14. **BECAUSE OF GOD'S "PERSECUTION":** Therefore they that were scattered abroad went every where preaching the word. - Acts 8:4

   If we do not fulfill Acts 1:8 (and ye shall be witnesses), then we may have to live to experience Acts 8:1 (And at that time there was a great persecution against the church which was at Jerusalem; and they were all scattered abroad...).

There is a great distance between "said" and "done."

THE PERPLEXITY IN PERSONAL EVANGELISM

ROMAN CATHOLICISM

1. **THE PRIESTHOOD**

    a. Jesus' death has done away with the Jewish Priesthood and sacrifices for sins. As such, there are no more priests needed to offer sacrifices for our sins in the New Testament churches.

        i. The New Testament has no priests in the church, only apostles, pastors, elders, bishops and evangelists.

            And he gave some, apostles; and some, prophets; and some, evangelists; and some, pastors and teachers; For the perfecting of the saints, for the work of the ministry, for the edifying of the body of Christ. - Eph 4:11-12

            And when they had ordained them elders in every church... - Acts 14:23 / Paul and Timotheus, the servants of Jesus Christ, to all the saints in Christ Jesus which are at Philippi, with the bishops and deacons. - Phil 1:1 / This is a true saying, If a man desire the office of a bishop, he desireth a good work. - 1 Tim 3:1 / The elders which are among you I (Peter) exhort, who am also an elder... - 1 Pet 5:1

        ii. Jesus' death has done away with the system of sacrifices in the church.

            Who needeth not daily, as those high priests, to offer up sacrifice, first for his own sins, and then for the people's: for this he did once, when he offered up himself. - Heb 7:27

            By the which will we are sanctified through the offering of the body of Jesus Christ once for all... For by one offering he hath perfected for ever them that are sanctified. - Heb 10:10-14

            Now where remission (forgiveness) of these is, there is no more offering for sin. - Heb 10:18

Heresy is picking out what you want to believe and rejecting, or at least ignoring the rest. - A. W. Tozer

iii. The supernatural tearing of the veil in the Temple shows us that there is no more need for man to approach God through the system of the priesthood.

Once a year, on the Day of Atonement, the Jewish high priest would enter through the veil of the Temple into the Holy of holies to atone for the sins of the whole nation. When the Lord Jesus Christ died on the cross, the veil was supernaturally torn apart signifying that believers could now approach God directly through the Mediator, the Lord Jesus Christ. From that time onwards, the Old Testament priesthood and sacrifices for sins ceased. Unfortunately, Roman Catholicism has "sewn back the veil" and demanded that her followers once again approach God through the human priesthood.

Jesus, when he had cried again with a loud voice, yielded up the ghost. And, behold, the veil of the temple was rent in twain from the top to the bottom; and the earth did quake, and the rocks rent. - Mt 27:50-51

And after the second veil, the tabernacle which is called the Holiest of all... but by his own blood he entered in once into the holy place, having obtained eternal redemption for us. - Heb 9:3-12

b. Every believer, through Christ, is now a spiritual priest of God.

i. Ye also, as lively stones, are built up a spiritual house, an holy priesthood, to offer up spiritual sacrifices, acceptable to God by Jesus Christ... But ye are a chosen generation, a royal priesthood, an holy nation, a peculiar people; that ye should shew forth the praises of him who hath called you out of darkness into his marvellous light. - 1 Pet 2:5,9

c. God wants us to approach Him personally through the Lord Jesus Christ who is meek and lowly in heart and turns no one away. The Bible does not teach us to seek God through the priesthood of Catholicism for forgiveness of sins or for blessing.

The most dangerous of all false doctrine is the one seasoned with a little truth.

i.   For there is one God, and one mediator between God and men, the man Christ Jesus (not Mary, the priests or the saints). - 1 Tim 2:5

ii.   ... And if any man sin, we have an advocate with the Father, Jesus Christ the righteous (not Mary, the priests or the saints). - 1 Jn 2:1

iii.   Wherefore he is able also to save them to the uttermost that come unto God by him, seeing he ever liveth to make intercession for them. - Heb 7:25

iv.   For we have not an high priest which cannot be touched with the feeling of our infirmities; but was in all points tempted like as we are, yet without sin. Let us therefore come boldly unto the throne of grace, that we may obtain mercy, and find grace to help in time of need. - Heb 4:15-16

v.   If we confess our sins, he is faithful and just to forgive us our sins, and to cleanse us from all unrighteousness. - 1 Jn 1:9

vi.   Come unto me (not Mary, the priests or the saints), all ye that labour and are heavy laden, and I will give you rest. Take my yoke upon you, and learn of me; for I am meek and lowly in heart: and ye shall find rest unto your souls. - Mt 11:28-29

vii.   All that the Father giveth me shall come to me; and him that cometh to me (not Mary, the priests or the saints) I will in no wise cast out. - Jn 6:37

d.   Roman Catholic priests ought to be married.

    i.   **PETER WAS MARRIED:** And when Jesus was come into Peter's house, he saw his wife's mother laid, and sick of a fever. - Mt 8:14

    ii.   **THE APOSTLES WERE MARRIED:** Have we not power to lead about a sister, a wife, as well as other apostles, and as the brethren of the Lord, and Cephas? - 1 Cor 9:5

iii. **THE BISHOP OUGHT TO BE MARRIED:** A bishop then must be blameless, the husband of one wife, vigilant, sober, of good behaviour, given to hospitality, apt to teach... One that ruleth well his own house, having his children in subjection with all gravity; (For if a man know not how to rule his own house, how shall he take care of the church of God?) - 1 Tim 3:2-5

iv. **THE ELDERS OUGHT TO BE MARRIED:** ... and ordain elders in every city, as I had appointed thee: If any be blameless, the husband of one wife, having faithful children not accused of riot or unruly. - Tit 1:5-6

v. **FORCED CELIBACY IS A DOCTRINE OF THE DEVIL:** Now the Spirit speaketh expressly, that in the latter times some shall depart from the faith, giving heed to seducing spirits, and doctrines of devils; Speaking lies in hypocrisy; having their conscience seared with a hot iron; Forbidding to marry, and commanding to abstain from meats, which God hath created to be received with thanksgiving of them which believe and know the truth. - 1 Tim 4:1-3

vi. Most of the apostles, including Peter, were married. In fact, the Bible encouraged the men of God to be married and raise their families in the way of God. Their ability to control their family was the criteria for their calling into the pastorate. In the Bible, celibacy is voluntary and forced celibacy is a doctrine of the devils. In addition, the Catholic Church teaches that marriage is a sacrament which confers merits on the recipients and, in the same breath, declares that it is forbidden to the priesthood.

e. We cannot address the priest as our spiritual "father".

i. And call no man your father upon the earth: for one is your Father, which is in heaven. - Mt 23:9

ii. We may address our biological fathers as "father" but we cannot address the priests as our spiritual "fathers" as there is only one spiritual Father, that is, God - "... Our Father which art in heaven, Hallowed be thy name." (Mt 6:9)

A man may go to hell as well for heresy as for adultery. - Thomas Watson

     iii.   The word "Pope" means "father".

2.   PETER AND THE PAPACY.

a.   Peter is not the "Rock" of the Church, Christ is.

    i.   And I say also unto thee, That thou art Peter (Petros, a stone), and upon this rock (Petra, the Lord Jesus, a Massie Rock) I will build my church; and the gates of hell shall not prevail against it. - Mt 16:18

    ii.   For other foundation can no man lay than that is laid, which is Jesus Christ. - 1 Cor 3:11

    iii.   And are built upon the foundation of the apostles and prophets, Jesus Christ himself being the chief corner stone. - Eph 2:20

    iv.   ... Behold, I lay in Sion a chief corner stone, elect, precious: and he that believeth on him shall not be confounded. - 1 Pet 2:6

b.   Peter did not exclusively have the "keys" to the Kingdom of Heaven.

    i.   **PETER HAD THE "KEYS"**: And I will give unto thee the keys of the kingdom of heaven: and whatsoever thou shalt bind on earth shall be bound in heaven: and whatsoever thou shalt loose on earth shall be loosed in heaven. - Mt 16:19

       Peter had the privilege to open the door of the gospel to: the Jews (Acts 2), Samaritans (Acts 8:5-17) and the Gentiles (Acts 10) This was in accordance to the Great Commission: "But ye shall receive power, after that the Holy Ghost is come upon you: and ye shall be witnesses unto me both in Jerusalem, and in all Judaea, and in Samaria, and unto the uttermost part of the earth." (Acts 1:8

ii. **THE CHURCH TODAY COLLECTIVELY HAS THE "KEYS":** ... And if he shall neglect to hear them, tell it unto the church: but if he neglect to hear the church, let him be unto thee as an heathen man and a publican. Verily I say unto you, Whatsoever ye shall bind on earth shall be bound in heaven: and whatsoever ye shall loose on earth shall be loosed in heaven. - Mt 18:15-18

c. Peter was not infallible.

    i. But he turned, and said unto Peter, Get thee behind me, Satan: thou art an offence unto me: for thou savourest not the things that be of God, but those that be of men. - Mt 16:23

    ii. But when Peter was come to Antioch, I withstood him to the face, because he was to be blamed. - Gal 2:11

d. Peter did not make claims to be the Pope of the Church nor seek obeisance from man.

    i. And as Peter was coming in, Cornelius met him, and fell down at his feet, and worshipped him. But Peter took him up, saying, Stand up; I myself also am a man. - Acts 10:25-26

    ii. The elders which are among you I (Peter) exhort, who am also an elder (a pastor among pastors), and a witness of the sufferings of Christ, and also a partaker of the glory that shall be revealed. - 1 Pet 5:1

e. Peter was married even as an apostle.

    i. ... And Simon's wife's mother was taken with a great fever; and they besought him for her. - Lk 4:38

    ii. Have we not power to lead about a sister, a wife, as well as other apostles, and as the brethren of the Lord, and Cephas (Peter)? - 1 Cor 9:5

152   The greatest mystery in Roman Catholicism: How can one be unmarried when he has a mother-in-law?

3. **THE MASS**

   a. The Lord's Supper is an ordinance of remembrance and not a sacrament (something that bestows merit to sinners to help save them from hell).

      i. And when he had given thanks, he brake it, and said, Take, eat: this is my body, which is broken for you: this do in remembrance of me (not for salvation). After the same manner also he took the cup, when he had supped, saying, This cup is the new testament in my blood: this do ye, as oft as ye drink it, in remembrance of me. - 1 Cor 11:24-25

   b. The elements of the Lord's Supper remain unchanged after consecration.

      i. For as often as ye eat this bread, and drink this cup (not the literal body and blood of Christ), ye do shew the Lord's death till he come. - 1 Cor 11:26

      ii. To the average Roman Catholic, the elements of the Mass after consecration, literally transform into the body and blood of Christ (transubstantiation). However, Paul asserted that, even after the blessings were given for the elements, they remained as the unleaven bread and fruit of the vine - unchanged.

   c. There is no need for the repeated sacrifices of Christ prescribed in the Mass.

      i. Who needeth not daily, as those high priests, to offer up sacrifice, first for his own sins, and then for the people's: for this he did once, when he offered up himself. - Heb 7:27

      ii. Nor yet that he should offer himself often, as the high priest entereth into the holy place every year with blood of others; For then must he often have suffered since the foundation of the world... - Heb 9:25-26

      iii. By the which will we are sanctified through the offering of the body of Jesus Christ once for all.

And every priest standeth daily ministering and offering oftentimes the same sacrifices, which can never take away sins: But this man, after he had offered one sacrifice for sins for ever, sat down on the right hand of God... For by one offering he hath perfected for ever them that are sanctified. - Heb 10:10-14

iv. Now where remission of these is, there is no more offering for sin. - Heb 10:18

v. Each time the Catholic Mass is performed, it is a bloodless sacrifice of Christ for our sins all over again. However, the Scriptures tell us that Christ's death is a once-for-all event never to be repeated.

4. MARY

a. Mary is not the "Mother of God."

i. And when they wanted wine, the mother of Jesus saith unto him, They have no wine. Jesus saith unto her, Woman, what have I to do with thee? mine hour is not yet come. - Jn 2:3-4

ii. When Jesus therefore saw his mother, and the disciple standing by, whom he loved, he saith unto his mother, Woman, behold thy son! - Jn 19:26

iii. When the Lord Jesus came of age, He would not address Mary as "mother" but "woman" as He did with other women. Mary was the physical mother of the Lord Jesus but not His spiritual or heavenly "mother".

b. Mary's given title "The Queen of Heaven" by the Roman Catholics is the title of a paganistic goddess.

i. The children gather wood, and the fathers kindle the fire, and the women knead their dough, to make cakes to the queen of heaven, and to pour out drink offerings unto other gods, that they may provoke me to anger. - Jer 7:18

It always takes a theologian to miss the point.

c. Mary too, was a sinner like all of us.

    i. And my spirit hath rejoiced in God my Saviour. - Lk 1:47

    ii. ... And to offer a sacrifice according to that which is said in the law of the Lord, A pair of turtledoves, or two young pigeons. - Lk 2:22-24

    iii. ... And if she be not able to bring a lamb, then she shall bring two turtles, or two young pigeons; the one for the burnt offering, and the other for a sin offering: and the priest shall make an atonement for her, and she shall be clean. - Lev 12:6-8

    iv. Wherefore, as by one man sin entered into the world, and death by sin; and so death passed upon all men (including Mary), for that all have sinned. - Rom 5:12

    v. In addressing God as Saviour, she acknowledged that she too, was a sinner like us. Her offerings to the Temple after the birth of the Lord Jesus were an offering for her sins. If Mary had to be sinless to conceive the Lord Jesus Christ, then the mother of Mary too, had to be sinless to conceive a sinless Mary, et al.

d. Mary is not our Mediator, Jesus is.

    i. For there is one God, and one mediator between God and men, the man Christ Jesus (not Mary). - 1 Tim 2:5

    ii. ... And if any man sin, we have an advocate with the Father, Jesus Christ the righteous (not Mary). - 1 Jn 2:1

    iii. ... It is Christ that died, yea rather, that is risen again, who is even at the right hand of God, who also maketh intercession for us (not Mary). - Rom 8:34

    iv. Wherefore he is able also to save them to the uttermost that come unto God by him, seeing he ever liveth to make intercession for them. - Heb 7:25

The main object of religion is not to get a man into heaven, but to get heaven into him.

v. Roman Catholics have been taught that God or Jesus Christ is a little unapproachable and Mary, being a woman and a mother, is more approachable. Whatever we desire, we should approach her and she, in turn, will petition her son, Jesus Christ, to give us our requests. On the contrary, the Bible tells us to approach God directly through the merits of the Lord Jesus Christ who is our Mediator, Intercessor and Advocate. The Roman Catholics unfortunately have replaced an approachable, meek and lowly Jesus with an imaginary "Mary, the Mother of God."

vi. A Romanist soldier was lying wounded in France, when a chaplain went near him, and the wounded man said, "I don't want you - you don't believe in 'Our Mother.'" Said the chaplain, "We respect Mary as the mother of our Lord, but you look as if you need the doctor." "Yes," said the man. The chaplain answered, "Will you have the doctor, or the doctor's mother?" We need Jesus Christ, the great Physician, more than His mother. - Christian Herald

e. Mary was not a perpetual virgin. She had other children after the birth of the Lord Jesus Christ.

i. Then Joseph... knew her not till she had brought forth her firstborn son: and he called his name JESUS. - Mt 1:24-25

This implies that Joseph and Mary did lead a normal married life after the birth of the Lord Jesus Christ.

ii. Is not this the carpenter's son? is not his mother called Mary? and his brethren, James, and Joses, and Simon, and Judas? And his sisters, are they not all with us? Whence then hath this man all these things? - Mt 13:55-56

iii. These all continued with one accord in prayer and supplication, with the women, and Mary the mother of Jesus, and with his brethren. - Acts 1:14

iv. But other of the apostles saw I none, save James the Lord's brother. - Gal 1:19

"Being on the Lord's side is more important than arrogantly assuming He is on your side." - President Abraham Lincoln

f. Mary is not to be prayed to, only God.

    i. And whatsoever ye shall ask in my name (not Mary), that will I do, that the Father may be glorified in the Son. - Jn 14:13

    ii. Hitherto have ye asked nothing in my name (not Mary): ask, and ye shall receive, that your joy may be full. - Jn 16:24

    iii. He that spared not his own Son, but delivered him up for us all, how shall he not with him (not Mary) also freely give us all things? - Rom 8:32

g. Christ views obedience more important than physical kinship with Him.

    i. And it came to pass, as he spake these things, a certain woman of the company lifted up her voice, and said unto him, Blessed is the womb that bare thee, and the paps which thou hast sucked. But he said, Yea rather, blessed are they that hear the word of God, and keep it. - Lk 11:27-28

5. SAINTS AND IMAGES

a. We cannot make them or bow ourselves to them.

    i. Thou shalt not make unto thee any graven image, or any likeness of any thing that is in heaven above, or that is in the earth beneath, or that is in the water under the earth: Thou shalt not bow down thyself to them, nor serve them: for I the LORD thy God am a jealous God, visiting the iniquity of the fathers upon the children unto the third and fourth generation of them that hate me - Exod 20:4-5

    ii. Ye shall make you no idols nor graven image, neither rear you up a standing image, neither shall ye set up any image of stone in your land, to bow down unto it: for I am the LORD your God. - Lev 26:1

    iii. Cursed be the man that maketh any graven or molten image, an abomination unto the LORD, the work of the hands of the craftsman, and putteth it in a secret place. And all the people shall answer and say, Amen. - Deut 27:15

  b. All true believers, living or dead, are called saints.

    i. Unto the church of God which is at Corinth, to them that are sanctified in Christ Jesus, called to be saints... - 1 Cor 1:2

    ii. Paul, an apostle of Jesus Christ by the will of God, to the saints which are at Ephesus, and to the faithful in Christ Jesus. - Eph 1:1

    iii. Paul and Timotheus, the servants of Jesus Christ, to all the saints in Christ Jesus which are at Philippi, with the bishops and deacons. - Phil 1:1

  c. The Lord Jesus Christ, not the Catholic "saints", is our intercessor with God.

    i. For there is one God, and one mediator between God and men, the man Christ Jesus. - 1 Tim 2:5

6. PURGATORY

  a. All believers are saved immediately and completely.

    i. And brought them out, and said, Sirs, what must I do to be saved? And they said, Believe on the Lord Jesus Christ, and thou shalt be saved, and thy house. - Acts 16:30-31

    ii. That if thou shalt confess with thy mouth the Lord Jesus, and shalt believe in thine heart that God hath raised him from the dead, thou shalt be saved. - Rom 10:9

    iii. Verily, verily, I say unto you, He that heareth my word, and believeth on him that sent me, hath everlasting life, and shall not come into condemnation; but is passed from death unto life. - Jn 5:24

A good life fears not life nor death. - Thomas Fuller

iv. For by one offering he hath perfected for ever them that are sanctified. - Heb 10:14

v. He that hath the Son hath life; and he that hath not the Son of God hath not life. These things have I written unto you that believe on the name of the Son of God; that ye may know that ye have eternal life, and that ye may believe on the name of the Son of God. - 1 Jn 5:12-13

b. There is no purgatory in the Bible.

i. And Jesus said unto him, Verily I say unto thee, To day shalt thou be with me in paradise (not purgatory). - Lk 23:43

ii. We are confident, I say, and willing rather to be absent from the body, and to be present with the Lord (not purgatory). - 2 Cor 5:8

iii. There is therefore now no condemnation (including no purgatory) to them which are in Christ Jesus, who walk not after the flesh, but after the Spirit. - Rom 8:1

iv. And God shall wipe away all tears from their eyes; and there shall be no more death, neither sorrow, nor crying, neither shall there be any more pain: for the former things are passed away. - Rev 21:4

c. Prayers for the dead in purgatory are condemned.

i. Woe unto you, scribes and Pharisees, hypocrites! for ye devour widows' houses, and for a pretence make long prayer: therefore ye shall receive the greater damnation. - Mt 23:14

ii. For the saved in heaven, prayers are not needed. For the lost in hell, prayers cannot help. No priest or pope knows when a deceased Roman Catholic has left purgatory. The living Catholic has to keep on paying for the endless masses to be said for the dead.

Low money, low mass;

High money, high mass;

No money, no mass. - Italian joke

7.   **PENANCE**

   a.   The Bible teaches repentance, not penance.

      i.   If we confess our sins, he is faithful and just to forgive us our sins, and to cleanse us from all unrighteousness. - 1 Jn 1:9

      ii.   And that repentance (not penance) and remission of sins should be preached in his name among all nations, beginning at Jerusalem. - Lk 24:47

      iii.   ... Woman, where are those thine accusers? hath no man condemned thee? She said, No man, Lord. And Jesus said unto her, Neither do I condemn thee: go, and sin no more (not do penance). - Jn 8:10-11

      iv.   After confessing their sins to the priests and receiving forgiveness through them, the penitent Roman Catholics still have to do the works prescribed by the priests like saying "Hail Mary" a hundred times. Such practices cannot be found in the Bible.

8.   **HUMAN TRADITIONS**

   a.   Human traditions add and subtract from the Word of God.

      i.   For I testify unto every man that heareth the words of the prophecy of this book, If any man shall add unto these things, God shall add unto him the plagues that are written in this book: And if any man shall take away from the words of the book of this prophecy, God shall take away his part out of the book of life, and out of the holy city, and from the things which are written in this book. - Rev 22:18-19

   b.   Those who follow human traditions and not the Word of God have no eternal life.

160

The wise man adjusts himself to the Bible, the fool adjusts the Bible to himself.

i. ... But he answered and said unto them, Why do ye also transgress the commandment of God by your tradition?... Thus have ye made the commandment of God of none effect by your tradition. Ye hypocrites, well did Esaias prophesy of you, saying, This people draweth nigh unto me with their mouth, and honoureth me with their lips; but their heart is far from me. But in vain they do worship me, teaching for doctrines the commandments of men. - Mt 15:1-9

ii. To the law and to the testimony: if they speak not according to this word, it is because there is no light in them. - Isa 8:20

c. Some examples of Catholic traditions which cannot be supported by the Scriptures.

   i. Prayers for the dead and making the sign of the cross - approx 310 AD

   ii. Veneration for the angels and dead saints - approx 320 AD

   iii. The Mass - approx 394 AD

   iv. The Worship of Mary - approx 431 AD

   v. The doctrine of Purgatory - approx 593 AD

   vi. Holy Water - approx 850 AD

   vii. Canonization of the dead saints - approx 995 AD

   viii. Fasting on Fridays and during Lent - approx 998 AD

   ix. Confession to priests - approx 1215 AD

   x. Immaculate Conception of Virgin Mary - approx 1854 AD

9. THE JESUS OF THE ROMAN CATHOLICS.

a. The "Jesus Christ" of the Roman Catholics:

   i. **HE IS UNABLE:** Roman Catholicism is a system of the doing of good works and acquiring of merits to get into heaven. As such, it shows that their "Jesus Christ" did not pay for their sins completely. If their "Jesus Christ" died for all their sins, then there should be no purgatory to pay for their "unpaid sins."

    ii.   **HE IS UNAPPROACHABLE:** Roman Catholics are encouraged to pray to Mother Mary because she, being a woman, is more compassionate and approachable.

b.   The Jesus Christ of the Bible.

    i.   **HE IS ABLE:**

For by one offering he hath perfected for ever them that are sanctified. - Heb 10:14

These things have I written unto you that believe on the name of the Son of God; that ye may know that ye have eternal life, and that ye may believe on the name of the Son of God. - 1 Jn 5:13

The Jesus Christ of the Bible came to save us completely. He died to pay for our sins - past, present and future.

    ii.   **HE IS APPROACHABLE:**

Come unto me, all ye that labour and are heavy laden, and I will give you rest... for I am meek and lowly in heart: and ye shall find rest unto your souls. - Mt 11:28-29

All that the Father giveth me shall come to me; and him that cometh to me I will in no wise cast out. - Jn 6:37

c.   If we believe in the wrong "Jesus Christ", we have no eternal life.

    i.   For there shall arise false Christs, and false prophets, and shall shew great signs and wonders; insomuch that, if it were possible, they shall deceive the very elect. - Mt 24:24

    ii.   For many shall come in my name, saying, I am Christ; and shall deceive many. - Mt 24:5

If Jesus Christ is not true God, how could he help us? If he is not true man, how could he help us? - Dietrich Bonhoeffer

10. SALVATION

a. Salvation in the Bible is purely by faith and not of works.

   i. For by grace are ye saved through faith; and that not of yourselves: it is the gift of God: Not of works, lest any man should boast. - Eph 2:8-9

   ii. And if by grace, then is it no more of works: otherwise grace is no more grace. But if it be of works, then is it no more grace: otherwise work is no more work. - Rom 11:6

   iii. But that no man is justified by the law in the sight of God, it is evident: for, The just shall live by faith. - Gal 3:11

b. Salvation by good works makes a lost man.

   i. What shall we say then? That the Gentiles, which followed not after righteousness, have attained to righteousness, even the righteousness which is of faith. But Israel, which followed after the law of righteousness, hath not attained to the law of righteousness. Wherefore? Because they sought it not by faith, but as it were by the works of the law. For they stumbled at that stumblingstone. - Rom 9:30-32

   ii. For as many as are of the works of the law are under the curse: for it is written, Cursed is every one that continueth not in all things which are written in the book of the law to do them. But that no man is justified by the law in the sight of God, it is evident: for, The just shall live by faith. And the law is not of faith: but, The man that doeth them shall live in them. Christ hath redeemed us from the curse of the law, being made a curse for us: for it is written, Cursed is every one that hangeth on a tree. - Gal 3:10-13

   iii. Christ is become of no effect unto you, whosoever of you are justified by the law; ye are fallen from grace. - Gal 5:4

iv. The basic and fatal error of Romanism is the denial of the sufficiency of Christ as Saviour. Romanism has a Christ, but He is not sufficient as a Saviour. What He did on Calvary must be repeated (in the mass) and supplemented (through works of penance), and this makes priestcraft and sacramentarianism necessary. It offers salvation on the installment plan, and then sees to it that the poor sinner is always behind in his payments, so that when he dies there is a large balance unpaid, and he must continue payments by sufferings in purgatory, or until the debt is paid by prayers, alms and sufferings of his living relatives and friends. The whole system and plan calls for merit and money. - Dr. C. D. Cole

v. Many will say to me in that day, Lord, Lord, have we not prophesied in thy name? and in thy name have cast out devils? and in thy name done many wonderful works? And then will I profess unto them, I never knew you: depart from me, ye that work iniquity. - Mt 7:22-23

The religion of the Bible is a religion of grace or it is nothing.
- James Moffat

THE PLAN IN PERSONAL EVANGELISM

CREATION AND THE CREATOR

1. For the invisible things of him from the creation of the world are clearly seen, being understood by the things that are made, even his eternal power and Godhead; so that they are without excuse. - Rom 1:20

2. The heavens declare the glory of God; and the firmament sheweth his handiwork. - Psa 19:1

3. All things were made by him; and without him was not any thing made that was made. - Jn 1:3

4. For every house is builded by some man; but he that built all things is God. - Heb 3:4

5. He was in the world, and the world was made by him, and the world knew him not. - Jn 1:10

6. The fool hath said in his heart, There is no God. - Psa 14:1

SIN AND THE SINNER

1. For all have sinned, and come short of the glory of God. - Rom 3:23

2. For there is not a just man upon earth, that doeth good, and sinneth not. - Eccl 7:20

3. But we are all as an unclean thing, and all our righteousnesses are as filthy rags... - Isa 64:6

4. Therefore to him that knoweth to do good, and doeth it not, to him it is sin. - Jas 4:17

5. For from within, out of the heart of men, proceed evil thoughts, adulteries, fornications, murders, Thefts, covetousness, wickedness, deceit, lasciviousness, an evil eye, blasphemy, pride, foolishness: All these evil things come from within, and defile the man. - Mk 7:21-23

6. Shapen in iniquity - Psa 51:5 / Fools make a mock at sin - Prov 14:9 / Can the Ethiopian change his skin - Jer 13:23 / To lust after her hath committed adultery - Mt 5:28 / He that is without sin among you, let him first cast a stone at her - Jn 8:1-9 / Being filled with all unrighteousness - Rom 1:28-32 / For that all have sinned - Rom 5:12

DEATH AND THE JUDGMENT OF GOD

1. <u>For the wages of sin is death</u>; but the gift of God is eternal life through Jesus Christ our Lord. - Rom 6:23

2. <u>And as it is appointed unto men once to die</u>, but after this the judgment. - Heb 9:27

3. <u>Be not deceived; God is not mocked</u>: for whatsoever a man soweth, that shall he also reap. - Gal 6:7

4. <u>The wicked shall be turned into hell</u>, and all the nations that forget God. - Psa 9:17

5. <u>The soul that sinneth, it shall die...</u> - Ezek 18:20

6. <u>... for there is nothing covered</u>, that shall not be revealed; and hid, that shall not be known. - Mt 10:26

7. <u>And fear not them which kill the body</u>, but are not able to kill the soul: but rather fear him which is able to destroy both soul and body in hell. - Mt 10:28

8. <u>And shall cast them into the furnace of fire</u>: there shall be wailing and gnashing of teeth. - Mt 13:50

9. <u>For what shall it profit a man</u>, if he shall gain the whole world, and lose his own soul? Or what shall a man give in exchange for his soul? - Mk 8:36-37

10. Fire that never shall be quenched - Mk 9:43-44 / The rich man and Lazarus - Lk 16:19-31 / Men loved darkness rather than light - Jn 3:19-20 / Sinned without law shall also perish without law - Rom 2:12-16 / Shall keep the whole law, and yet offend in one point - Jas 2:10 / The dead, small and great, stand before God - Rev 20:12-15 / The second death - Rev 21:8

To be alone with my conscience is hell enough for me. - Shakespeare

GOD'S LOVE AND PROVISION

1. <u>But God commendeth his love toward us,</u> in that, while we were yet sinners, Christ died for us. - Rom 5:8

2. <u>For the Son of man is come to seek and to save that which was lost.</u> - Lk 19:10

3. <u>For God so loved the world, that he gave his only begotten Son,</u> that whosoever believeth in him should not perish, but have everlasting life. For God sent not his Son into the world to condemn the world; but that the world through him might be saved. - Jn 3:16-17

4. <u>Greater love hath no man than this,</u> that a man lay down his life for his friends. - Jn 15:13

5. <u>But he was wounded for our transgressions, he was bruised for our iniquities:</u> the chastisement of our peace was upon him; and with his stripes we are healed. All we like sheep have gone astray; we have turned every one to his own way; and the LORD hath laid on him the iniquity of us all. - Isa 53:5-6

6. <u>For I delivered unto you first of all that which I also received,</u> how that Christ died for our sins according to the scriptures; And that he was buried, and that he rose again the third day according to the scriptures. - 1 Cor 15:3-4

7. But we see Jesus, who was made a little lower than the angels for the suffering of death, crowned with glory and honour; <u>that he by the grace of God should taste death for every man.</u> - Heb 2:9

8. And almost all things are by the law purged with blood; <u>and without shedding of blood is no remission.</u> - Heb 9:22

9. <u>And he is the propitiation for our sins:</u> and not for ours only, but also for the sins of the whole world. - 1 Jn 2:2

10. <u>Who will have all men to be saved,</u> and to come unto the knowledge of the truth. - 1 Tim 2:4

Go and toil in any vineyard. Do not fear to do or dare. If you want a field of labor, you can find it anywhere.

SALVATION BY FAITH IN JESUS CHRIST

1. <u>That if thou shalt confess with thy mouth the Lord Jesus, and shalt believe in thine heart that God hath raised him from the dead, thou shalt be saved</u>. - Rom 10:9

2. <u>Jesus saith unto him, I am the way, the truth, and the life</u>: no man cometh unto the Father, but by me. - Jn 14:6

3. <u>Verily, verily, I say unto you, He that heareth my word, and believeth on him that sent me, hath everlasting life</u>, and shall not come into condemnation; but is passed from death unto life. - Jn 5:24

4. <u>... Sirs, what must I do to be saved</u>? And they said, Believe on the Lord Jesus Christ, and thou shalt be saved, and thy house. - Acts 16:30-31

5. <u>For by grace are ye saved through faith</u>; and that not of yourselves: it is the gift of God: Not of works, lest any man should boast. - Eph 2:8-9

6. <u>As far as the east is from the west</u>, so far hath he removed our transgressions from us. - Psa 103:12

7. <u>Therefore if any man be in Christ, he is a new creature</u>: old things are passed away; behold, all things are become new. - 2 Cor 5:17

8. <u>Behold, I stand at the door, and knock</u>: if any man hear my voice, and open the door, I will come in to him, and will sup with him, and he with me. - Rev 3:20

9. Though your sins be as scarlet - Isa 1:18 / They that be whole need not a physician - Mt 9:12-13 / The prodigal son - Lk 15:11-24 / The Pharisee and the publican - Lk 18:9-14 / Whosoever believe in him should not perish - Jn 3:15-16 / Hath everlasting life - Jn 3:36 / The just shall live by faith - Rom 1:17 / Abraham believed God - Rom 4:2-8 / Justified by faith, we have peace - Rom 5:1 / They sought it not by faith - Rom 9:30-32 / No more of works - Rom 11:6 / Under

the curse - Gal 3:10 / No man is justified by the law - Gal 3:11 / Christ is become of no effect - Gal 5:4 / One mediator - 1 Tim 2:5 / Not by works of righteousness - Tit 3:5 / Cleanse us from all unrighteousness - 1 Jn 1:9 / He that hath the Son hath life - 1 Jn 5:12 / Ye have eternal life - 1 Jn 5:13

WHAT MUST YOU DO TO BE SAVED

1. **Repentance:** To repent is to have a change of view regarding our sins and be willing to give them up.

    a. I tell you, Nay: but except ye repent, ye shall all likewise perish. - Lk 13:3

    b. Bring forth therefore fruits meet for repentance - Mt 3:7-8 / Repent ye, and believe the gospel - Mk 1:15 / Repent ye therefore, and be converted, that your sins may be blotted out - Acts 3:19

2. **Acceptance:** To accept is to receive by faith the Lord Jesus Christ into our hearts to be our Savior.

    a. But as many as received him, to them gave he power to become the sons of God, even to them that believe on his name. - Jn 1:12

    b. That whosoever believeth in him should not perish, but have everlasting life - Jn 3:15-16 / And him that cometh to me I will in no wise cast out - Jn 6:37 / He that hath the Son hath life - 1 Jn 5:12-13

A SINNER'S PRAYER

Dear God, I know I am a sinner. Please forgive me of my sins and help me to forsake them. I thank you for sending the Lord Jesus Christ who died for my sins and rose again on the third day. Now, I accept the Lord Jesus Christ to be my Savior. Please help me to love and obey you from this day onwards. I thank you for saving me. In Jesus' name I pray. Amen.

Likewise, I say unto you, there is joy in the presence of the angels of God over one sinner that repenteth. - Lk 15:10

ASSURANCE OF SALVATION

1. For whosoever shall call upon the name of the Lord shall be saved. - Rom 10:13

2. But as many as received him, to them gave he power to become the sons of God, even to them that believe on his name. - Jn 1:12

3. All that the Father giveth me shall come to me; and him that cometh to me I will in no wise cast out. - Jn 6:37

4. These things have I written unto you that believe on the name of the Son of God; that ye may know that ye have eternal life, and that ye may believe on the name of the Son of God. - 1 Jn 5:13

5. Assurance... enables a child of God to feel that the great business of life is a settled business, the great debt a paid debt, the great disease a healed disease and the great work a finished work. - J. C. Ryle

SECURITY OF SALVATION

1. There is therefore now no condemnation to them which are in Christ Jesus, who walk not after the flesh, but after the Spirit. - Rom 8:1

2. And I give unto them eternal life: and they shall never perish, neither shall any man pluck them out of my hand. - Jn 10:28

3. Who are kept by the power of God through faith unto salvation ready to be revealed in the last time. - 1 Pet 1:5

4. Now unto him that is able to keep you from falling, and to present you faultless before the presence of his glory with exceeding joy. - Jude 24

5. In hope of eternal life, which God, that cannot lie, promised before the world began. - Tit 1:2

The whole debate as to whether salvation can be lost or not is reduced to: who is keeping us saved - God or us?

What is the Gospel according to You?

You are writing a Gospel,
A chapter each day,
By deeds that you do,
By words that you say.
Men read what you write,
Whether faithless or true,
Say! What is the gospel
According to you?

The Gospel Work

The work is solemn - do not trifle.
The task is difficult - do not relax.
The opportunity is brief - do not delay.
The path is narrow - do not wander.
The prize is glorious - do not faint.

This world is our passage not our portion. - Matthew Henry

Man's problem rises from the fact that he has not only lost the way,
but he has lost the address. - Nicolas Bardyaen

We know how many seeds there are in an apple but we do not know
how many apples there are in a seed.

175

Crowd Followers

Look at those Crowd Followers, now aren't they a bunch?
Following the crowd from breakfast to lunch.
Never asking, "Where are we going?"
Just riding the current wherever it's flowing.

They say to themselves, "Now this sure is a breeze,
Following the crowd is as easy as you please."
They never stop to consider where all this will end;
They just keep on following all of their friends.

Everyone else must know where we're heading,
So why should I do any fretting?
I'll just follow the crowd all day and all night.
I'm sure everything will turn out all right.

Everyone is laughing and having such fun,
Why, not following the crowd would really be dumb.
I really don't care where all this may end;
I just want to keep having fun with my friends.

But every road must come to an end.
The Crowd Followers too have to round the last bend.
And when they do they will come face to face
With the Creator and Designer of the whole human race.

And He'll not ask what the crowd has to say,
For each person will have to speak for themselves that day.
And when everything has been said and done,
The crowd again will march forward as one.

No one will, that day, want to follow their friends,
Because they know destruction will be their end.
But because they spent their life following the crowd,
On that final day no turning back will be allowed.

-- Author Unknown --

He who has no concern for his eternity is more than a fool
- he is a madman. - C. H. Spurgeon

Made in the USA
Columbia, SC
23 August 2023

22018703R00102